THE MEN WE BECAME

The Men We Became

MY FRIENDSHIP WITH
John F. Kennedy Jr.

ROBERT T. LITTELL

ST. MARTIN'S PRESS NEW YORK

B
Ken

www.stmartins.com

Design by Victoria Hartman

ISBN 0-312-32476-6
EAN 978-0312-32476-6

First Edition: June 2004

1   3   5   7   9   10   8   6   4   2

To Coco, Tate, and the Mighty Wee

CONTENTS

———

———

CONTENTS

ACKNOWLEDGMENTS

———

LOVE AND THANKS beyond words to Francesca Hayslett, my wife, friend, and a talented writer who helped turn my tales of friendship into a book. Boundless love to Colette and Tate, my children. Thanks to superagent Denise Marcil for her support, hard work, and extraordinarily good judgment; to my editor, Charlie Spicer, and publisher, Sally Richardson, for believing in the book I wanted to write and then making it better; to my great friend John Hare, for faith and philosophical ponderings to last a lifetime. Love and gratitude to my mother and stepfather, Connie and David Katz, and my sister, Linda Littell. To Brian Alexander, thanks for reminding me how to tell a story. For help, guidance, and inspiration of every kind, thanks to Todd and Jennifer Turchetta, Joy Konarski, Maura Kye, Mary-Kate Przybycien, Miriam Kazdin, Gary Ginsberg, Roseanne Brandon, James Murphy, Herman Besselink, Marshall Chambers, Dom Starsia, and the man who invented Jiffy Pop. And, of course, a prayer of thanks and gratitude to John, who's still bringing out the best in me.

———

SKYWRITING

———

IN ANCIENT GREECE, heroes who died were sent to the night sky, where they offered guidance and inspiration for those left on earth. We all have our own constellations, filled with the public and private heroes of our time. I am one of many people for whom the night sky changed on July 16, 1999, when the plane carrying John F. Kennedy Jr., his wife, Carolyn Bessette Kennedy, and her sister Lauren Bessette went down in the waters off Martha's Vineyard. Unexpected, unbelievable, unalterable. John had been my closest friend for twenty years. We were going to be buddies until we died. Of old age. But John didn't grow old, and I don't have my buddy anymore. All I've got is the memory of his friendship and two decades of stories.

In *The Secret Life of Bees*, Sue Monk Kidd writes, "Stories have to be told or they die, and when they die, we can't remember who we are or why we are here." I don't want the stories to die. John and I were friends from the age of eighteen to thirty-eight, the years when we became the men we became. In losing him, I lost a part of myself, a chunk of my past as well as a future that included him. So be it. Nobody can change the ugly facts. But neither can anyone take away that we lived so well together. Or that we built an honorable friendship. Or that I loved him like a brother. I still love him. And I miss him dearly. He was such a bright light that my world is a lot darker without him. An anonymous Chinese poet once said that to re-create something in words is like being alive twice. In that sense, this book is a memoir of a friendship and a resurrection of sorts, an effort to fix John's bright star in my own sky.

It's also a tribute to an unusually graceful and gifted man, someone who was famous from birth but who was never, in my view, credited for his best qualities. A lot has been written about John since his death, but I don't recognize my friend in most of it. Maybe that's normal. We see our friends in a special light. But maybe it's because those of us who were closest to John—and he had a lot of friends—have never spoken publicly about him. It was like an unspoken oath: Those who truly loved John were rabidly protective of his privacy. Now that he's gone, though, our private admiration falls short. I'm biased, sure, but the man deserves better. To endure, with great success, your entire life in the public eye and then be dragged, without recourse, through the mud upon your passing is an injustice. He was not a prince but something better, a good man and a much-loved friend. I think that's a story that should be told.

THE MEN WE BECAME

One

FIRST IMPRESSIONS

———

ON A SUNNY September afternoon in 1979, I stood at the water's edge of 1st Beach in Newport, Rhode Island. It was orientation week for the freshman class at Brown University, and we were on a school-sponsored outing. I'd spent the day swimming, playing football, and catching Frisbees. Happy and tired, I was soaking up the sun before we headed back to campus. Not far from me sat a handsome, bored-looking group, obviously private-school graduates. They were easy to spot: set off to themselves, a blasé tribe wearing Vuarnet sunglasses, untucked button-downs, and baggy shorts. Only one of them, a good-looking guy with an athlete's body and a head full of brown curls, seemed to be genuinely enjoying himself, swimming and horsing around in the water.

I had just graduated from the Lawrenceville School, an all-boys prep school in New Jersey, where I'd been a day student. I'd spent the summer in Venice Beach, California, surfing, drinking San Miguels, and hanging out until the sun went down. I thought I knew the beach better than anyone. So, being eighteen years old

———

and competitive, I'd used the day to establish my alpha-dog status among my new peers. I'd caught more passes, ridden more waves, and spiked more volleyballs than the next guy.

I looked nothing like the J. Crew ad seated near me. I was six foot two and weighed 210 pounds, built more like a Midwestern farm boy than an East Coast patrician. My hair was plastered with seaweed and I had a mouth full of stainless-steel orthodontic work. I realized later, to my horror, that there were flecks of seaweed—the exact same green as the yin/yang symbol on my board shorts—stuck in my braces. But none of that seemed to matter to the curly-haired fellow I'd noticed a few minutes before. He walked up to me, stuck out his hand, and said, "Yo, my name's John. What's yours?"

Matching his friendly tone, I answered, "Rob Littell," and we shook hands.

John and I swapped high-school war stories for half an hour or so. He'd gone to Andover, a storied prep school in Massachusetts. I told him I was playing lacrosse for Brown. He told me he'd never played a team sport but was thinking of trying rugby. We hit it off immediately. He was cool, funny, and restless. He laughed at my oddball sense of humor. I liked his good-natured confidence.

Someone blew a whistle and we filed back onto a bunch of old yellow school buses. Bouncing toward Providence, battling motion sickness and a carbon monoxide headache, I dimly heard my new roommate, Bradley Foerster, say that the guy I'd been talking with was John F. Kennedy Jr. This was news to me. I'd had no idea that he was at Brown or even that "he" was such a big deal. In high school I'd played sports. Period. If *People* magazine existed in those days, we didn't get it at our house. I muttered to Bradley that John seemed friendly enough and I returned to my nausea. I remember being vaguely proud of my ignorance.

The next time I saw John was the following week, at my dormitory on the north side of campus. I was returning from class one afternoon and found him penning a note on the little bulletin board I'd Velcroed to the wall of my cinder-block alcove. He'd stopped by to say hi, so I treated him to a sampling of the B-52's and the Talking Heads. I was glad to see him. We clashed immediately over music—I was into New Wave while John was a throwback, a purist who preferred rock 'n' roll to pop, and the Rolling Stones to everything—and argued happily for an hour. John told me to come by his room sometime, so a few days later I headed over there. I remember thinking it was like an experiment. I'd see how it felt: if it would be easy and fun, or awkward and not worth the effort.

John's room was a classic freshman dorm room. Furniture from the fifties, a rotary phone, two narrow twin beds, and a roommate seemingly chosen at random. The roommate, John Moubayed, was from Providence, a local guy with a perpetually slightly sheepish smile. He didn't get too involved in the whirl of attention around John. They had a live-and-let-live arrangement that seemed to work well enough.

When I arrived at his room, John put his "master recording" of Supertramp's *Breakfast in America* on the stereo. I still don't know what a "master recording" is, but it sounded better than my records did. I soon learned that—no surprise—there were a lot of perks to being famous. John constantly received freebies and upgrades and "master recordings" of Top 40 hits. It didn't faze him, though, partly because it had been the norm all his life. He certainly didn't go looking for freebies, accepting most gifts just to be polite.

We started to hang out together, doing the normal things kids do at college. We went to parties, drank beer, and played Frisbee. Sometimes we hung out at Toad Hall, the lacrosse fraternity. Although I didn't think about it at the time, John had other options besides drinking beer and meeting jocks. Within weeks of the beginning of classes, and before the social cement had set, I met John's cousin Kerry Kennedy, who was also at Brown, and her beautiful friend Nancy Richardson, who eventually married John's cousin and confidant, Bobby Kennedy. I recall a Wednesday conversation with them about the upcoming weekend. John and I had run into them at the Blue Room, the mid-campus coffee shop and center of social activity at Brown. After a bit of small talk, I asked Nancy, "What are you guys doing this weekend?"

She replied, "We're going to Virginia to ride horses. It should be fun." She added, "Do you want to come? I think John's going."

Shocked that anyone might opt out of a beer-soaked weekend at the local fraternities to go horseback riding in another state, I answered, perhaps a bit defensively, "We're going to Phi Psi."

John changed his weekend plans on the spot. Assuming a perfect lockjaw accent, he exclaimed, "To Phi Psi!" as if it were the fox at the end of the hunt. We all laughed. And that weekend John and I went to Phi Psi, an on-campus fraternity with a reputation for rowdy parties. He had cast his lot with the regular guys.

Later, when I knew him better, I learned that John worked hard to be a "regular guy." His friends weren't famous, he never asked for special treatment (though sometimes he got it anyway), and he loved being "one of the guys." As easily as he moved about in the aristocratic world he'd grown up in, he was never intrigued by it.

Freshman year friends. From left: John Hare, John Kennedy, Jeff Gradinger, Billy Way, Dee Richards, Kim Witherspoon, me (in the hat), and Mary Kahn. (Courtesy of Taylor Gray)

By the time I met him, he already knew that his fulfillment would come from less-privileged pursuits. It's not that he wanted to give up his fame, which was as familiar to him as air is to the rest of us. And he guarded his privacy. But he wanted to be able to walk down the street or ride his bike just like everyone else, whether he was recognized or not. He deserves credit for this: He was one of the most famous people on earth and he rode the subway, played in the park, and hung out with his friends in full view of the world. No bodyguards, no Secret Service, no subterfuge. By refusing to be a recluse, he forced people to give him some space. And he returned the favor by being a generous and gracious public figure.

But I digress. My point is that starting college wasn't easy for him. He had to reestablish his hard-won freedom all over again, at a new school, in a new city. Supposedly there were television news crews on campus the first day, filming John as he registered for classes. I hadn't met him yet, but I'm sure he hated that. He wanted to be a college kid, not a freak show.

Coincidentally, I arrived at school feeling out of sync myself. I'd had a wild ride from birth to eighteen. The short version: My parents divorced when I was seven, my father moving on to seventies-style bohemian freedom with my wonderful stepmother, Tina Sloan. Freedom was short-lived, though, followed by drugs, then serious mental illness. My mother remarried as soon as he left, and for a while I had a stepfather as well as a stepbrother my own age. I loved them both. They left when I was fourteen. Two years later, my real father—whom I didn't see much anymore, but still . . . —hurled himself off a sixteenth-floor balcony of the Hollywood Holiday Inn, a suicide. We were living in another house by then, with my mother's new boyfriend, though he didn't last. Over the years we were rich and we were poor. We moved often. By the age of eighteen, I'd lived in fourteen homes—not foster homes, mind you, and some of them would qualify as mansions. But I would have traded them all for a permanent tree house. By the time I got to school, I was certain that I was special for everything I'd been through.

John and I, despite the obvious differences, shared similarities that connected us quickly. We had both weathered turbulent childhoods and emerged with the confidence of survivors. Neither of us had a father, nor could we really talk about our fathers' deaths. We'd been raised by and with women—she-wolves, as I called our strong-willed mothers and brainy sisters. And we shared a belief in our own future greatness. John's destiny was thrust upon him at birth, when he became the first (and last) child born to a President-elect who was then assassinated. Mine was harder to explain, a genetic quirk maybe, or the resolve of a child determined to wrest control of his fate.

My big Teflon-coated ego was an important part of our fast friendship. Irreverent and cocky, I believed that I was John's equal or better. I could be wowed by the trappings of his lifestyle— maybe—but I felt I deserved just as good. I can't explain this and don't defend it; it's just the way I was. And John liked it. We found friendship easy. From the start, we were each other's best audience. We each knew the other to be hilarious, brave, and brilliant. That's one of the key conditions for male bonding—deep, unconditional admiration. Add a constant stream of well-intentioned abuse and you've got the recipe for a great friendship.

In 1979, the year we started college, the Kennedy name carried a lot of baggage—good or bad, depending on whom you talked to. My grandfather, who asked me maybe three questions during our twenty-five years together on earth, popped one of them during a Thanksgiving visit I made to Florida that year. He was an old-line WASP from Barrington Hills, Illinois, where he'd made his name and fortune in banking. Granddad spent his winters in Naples, Florida, and while we stood together on the porch of his beachside home, the old sage asked whom I'd met at Brown. I told him about my roommate, Bradley, about a couple of lacrosse players I'd fallen in with, and about Francesca Hayslett, a girl from Connecticut with whom I was fast falling in love. I also mentioned that I'd met John Kennedy Jr. Granddad's left eyebrow rose slowly above the dark frames of his Ray-Bans. "Those Kennedy boys are no good," he stated.

"Oh, really," I responded respectfully, uncertain what else to say. I admired my grandfather more than anyone else in the world.

A silence. Thirty seconds later, Aunt Lee, Granddad's wife, walked by and added, "Those Kennedy boys are a pack of drunken wolves. They're always crashing parties up and down the coast."

I didn't find this new information especially crushing. But clearly, in the view of the conservative WASPs from whose nest I had recently flown, the Kennedys were masqueraders at best. Indeed, Aunt Lee made clear that but for their moonshine fortune, the Kennedys would be chauffeurs, not the chauffeured.

I had a chance to run with the Kennedy wolf pack the following weekend, when John and I decided to take a road trip. John wanted to pay a visit to his cousin Timothy Shriver, who was attending Yale. Since he didn't have a car—his mother wouldn't let him have one until junior year—we loaded two sports duffels and a cooler of Budweiser on ice into my Mazda GLC. We wore our best rugby shirts, with real rubber buttons, to honor Timmy's position on the notoriously hard-partying Yale rugby squad. Then we hit the highway, visions of bar dancing, coed cohabitation, and *Animal House* revelry in our heads.

The truth began to dawn on us somewhere south of Mystic, Connecticut. We were rolling along the East Coast's big family driveway, I-95, when we realized that we were going to New Haven. Ostensibly the Gateway to New England, New Haven has all the charm of a bus depot (though it does have great pizza). And we were visiting a seminary student. Whatever hope we still held for a wild weekend was dashed when we pulled up in front of Timmy's house. A large, light-filled town house, it was clean, comfortable, and eerily quiet—there wasn't a leaf out of place on the genteel block. Timmy was living there with his girlfriend, Linda Potter, whom he married not long after graduating. We'd come to New Haven to visit a quietly studious, as-good-as-married minister.

The rest of the weekend was like the house: clean and quiet. Linda was the perfect hostess in a milk-and-cookies way. We didn't crack open the cooler. We didn't light up the town. We didn't even *get* to town. Instead, we had a glass of wine at dinner that evening, the four of us discussing apartheid as though part of a televised panel. We finished the night on the couch, watching TV and falling asleep before *Saturday Night Live* came on. My guess is that Timmy wasn't always so staid. But that weekend he chose to set a good example, giving John and me a glimpse of a quiet, purposeful campus life.

It wasn't until years later that I caught a glimpse of the wild side of the Kennedys, and there was no drunkenness or party-crashing involved. It was the summer of 1988 and John had invited Frannie and me to stay at the family compound in Hyannis Port, on Cape Cod. The family was getting ready to play one of their famously competitive touch football games. The whole gang was there, with most of the players piling out of Robert F. Kennedy Sr.'s household. His sons Joe, Michael, Bobby, and Max and Senator Ted Kennedy's son Patrick were on the lawn, along with anyone else with a strong set of front teeth. It was a beautiful Sunday morning and we were in high spirits. The instant that play started, though, things took a turn for the ferocious. During the first five minutes of the game there were three arguments, two shoving matches, and no scoring. The cousins' handsome faces, smiling just moments before, contorted into grimaces. We all played fiercely, victory momentarily more important than life itself. I'd never played this kind of game. I'm not even sure it was a game. It was more like a battlefield, an arena in which these brothers and cousins played out the complex rivalries and emotions that all families have, especially theirs. Two-hand touches became tackles. Tackles became pile-ons. And John seemed to be on the receiving end of most of the excess elbows and biting commentary. By the end, I was mentally exhausted. Instead of the usual post-victory elation, I felt as though I'd just lost a two-hour catfight. As John and I walked back into his mother's house, I said to him, "What a pack of assholes."

John responded laughingly, "*That* was a mellow game."

I believed him. These guys were true warriors. John took the most heat because of the position he held in the family. On one hand, he was the only son of the most accomplished member of an accomplished clan. He was also, without question, the media's favorite Kennedy: the "sexiest" one, the one who never got in trouble. On the other hand, John was something of an outsider within the Kennedy family. Though close to several of his cousins, especially Timmy Shriver, Bobby Kennedy, and Willie Smith, he had a slightly strained relationship with the tight-knit crew as a whole. He'd been raised outside of their Massachusetts world, kept apart by his protective and New York–based mother. She saw to it that her children were as independent as she was. It wasn't long after our game that Mrs. Onassis built her own home on Martha's Vineyard—close to the family, but separate. The Hyannis Port gang teased John not for lack of love but, in my opinion, out of envy. This didn't bother him a bit. He had the best of many worlds and he knew it.

———

As it turned out, we didn't need to take any road trips freshman year. Our visions of wild times and raucous behavior were easily satisfied by walking across campus to Wriston Quad, which on a Saturday night felt like Bourbon Street at Mardi Gras. Not long after our Ozzie-and-Harriet–like Yale excursion, John and I found ourselves at a recruiting party at Phi Psi, located right on Wriston Quad and reputed to throw the best-looking parties in the school. We were there at the invitation of Rich Wiese, a born-and-bred New Yorker and decathlete whose all-American face had recently been discovered by the Ford modeling agency. Rich was the president of Phi Psi and had recently, famously, hosted Brooke Shields on her college visit. We figured him for a girl magnet.

Although we weren't members yet, Phi Psi quickly became our gathering spot. One evening a group of us were hanging out in the Phi Psi TV room when our friend Billy Way blew in the door. He was followed by six attractive and evidently inebriated young women from Providence College. Billy, who'd attended Andover with John, was a tennis star from Bermuda with yellow eyes and a sly, sweet manner. Women found him irresistible. He had made love to more girls by his eighteenth birthday than most guys fantasize about in their whole lifetime. Billy began to introduce his new following to the rest of us, escorting the cutest girl over to John. He introduced them, first names only. They chatted for a minute or so before Billy circled back around. Sensing a lack of spark, he told the girl that she was talking to the late President's son. She lit up like a Christmas tree, as if this news changed everything. Looking John right in the eye, she said, "Prove it." Without changing his straight-faced expression, John stuck his hand in his back pocket and from his wallet produced his New York State driver's license. The girl, all business at that point, reviewed the license for a moment and then, with a Cheshire kitten's grin, stuffed her right hand down the front of John's pants and led him out of the room.

When you're eighteen years old, you can get into a lot of trouble when people respond to you like that. And it happened often enough. John's combination of fame, good looks, and charm had a weird effect on some people. An astounding number of women wanted to sleep with him. Some men kept their distance, too proud to risk looking starstruck. Others were instantly ingratiating. To his credit, John handled the attention well. He had an enthusiastic libido but almost always resisted the sexual opportunities that came his way, preferring real relationships. And with people who completely lost their balance around him, he knew how to be polite but distant.

I had a harder time with John's star power. Basically, it scared me, because I was looking for stability or nothing in my future relationships. These instant friendships that John was offered seemed too fleeting, too subject to change. And I wanted nothing to do with change. It's no coincidence that I met my future wife, Frannie, and my best friend, John, in my first week at Brown—one week out of the hotbed of a household I'd grown up in. But in the beginning, John's celebrity made me nervous, as though I couldn't trust things on their surface. I liked the guy, but I was wary of his public persona. I certainly didn't want to be a fawning admirer.

Instinctively, I held myself and John to a higher standard. At least that's how I saw it. In truth, I compensated for the possible imbalance in our friendship by being a prick. Mostly it was minor stuff, like making sure that I rode shotgun on any car trip (and he had to ride in the back) or that I got the biggest slice of pizza. I always took the A section of *The New York Times* first. I would never cancel a plan, even a dumb one, if John invited me to do something. Little things, but it was not the way most people treated John. It was months before I eased up. John understood what I was doing because he subtly cheered me on, coming closer each time I pushed his public self away. He had no use for fawning admirers, and I challenged him. Slowly, the two of us made a game out of defining and adhering to the rules of friendship. We demanded fair and equal treatment from each other. When his head got big, I'd tell him, usually in an acerbic and pointed fashion. When I was a jerk, he'd be the first to break the news. It took a while, but we ultimately built a solid bond far removed from the corrosive effects of celebrity.

Over the winter break that first year, my family and I visited New York City to see the tree at Rockefeller Center. It was Christmas Eve and at my request, we began at Trader Vic's, a legendary watering hole that used to be located in the basement of the Plaza. We started by sucking down a couple of Samoan fog cutters (the drinking age was still eighteen). Our discussion got louder and more animated as we kept drinking, things reaching a fevered pitch when Mom started in on the gardenia-topped tiki puka puka I'd ordered for her. Thoroughly inebriated by now, we made our way to the Ravelled Sleeve for a seven-thirty dinner reservation. No sooner were we seated than my mother abruptly stopped talking. Her face turned an odd shade of gray and she excused herself to the ladies' room. Linda, my sixteen-year-old sister, went down to check on her about ten minutes later. She returned to report, "Mom is lying on the bathroom floor and won't get up. She claims she's dying."

When Linda's snickering subsided, she and I went down to the ladies' room to visit our maker. It wasn't every day that Mom wound up drunk in a restaurant bathroom, and we wanted to enjoy the spectacle firsthand. I leaned over her prostrate body and kindly informed her that she was simply drunk. She, however, continued to insist that she was dying and requested to be taken to the hospital. We hauled her off the tiles and up the stairs with considerable difficulty. It wasn't so funny anymore. We drove to St. Luke's Hospital on Seventy-second Street, where Mom was admitted for alcohol poisoning. The doctor told us to come back in a couple of hours in the hope that she could recite the alphabet. With any luck, we could be home before Santa's rounds.

I have a phobia of hospitals (dangerous places, you can get seriously hurt in there) and wanted to escape as fast as possible. So I called John. It was Christmas Eve and all, but, well, I was feeling a bit blue. John got on the phone and, after ribbing me for my sorry family outing, yelled to his mom to ask if Linda and I could come over. I protested—weakly, I admit—and a few minutes later we were in a cab on our way to 1040 Fifth Avenue. A doorman wearing a green jacket, striped vest, and bow tie let us in. As we passed through the glass-and-wrought-iron doors, the hustle and din of the city magically disappeared, replaced by another world, one of soothing civility. The porter led us through the typically decked-out Upper East Side lobby—checkered brown marble floors, gilt-framed sketches of tall ships, and mahogany tables to rest one's Bergdorf bags on—to an elevator on the left side of the building. Upon reaching the twelfth floor, the elevator opened onto a small foyer appointed with an antique table and mirror. I loved that mirror, a generous touch that let you smooth your clothes and check your hair before entering the elegant household that Mrs. Onassis ran. Everything in the house was beautiful, so you might as well look your best.

Rough-hewn suburban jungle boy that I was, I rang the doorbell with excitement. It was Christmas Eve and I was on altogether new turf, but I didn't feel the least bit uncomfortable. Chalk it up to ego or ignorance or pure competitive spirit, but all I wanted to do was see my friend and check out his obviously cool apartment.

My sister and I heard someone inside bound across the apartment. John swung open the door, said, "C'mon," and headed toward his room, impatient to show off his stuff. Disarmed by John's lack of pretension, Linda and I followed him through the apartment. As far as I could tell, the household looked ready to turn in for the night, though it was only about nine. It was quiet, calm, the lights on the Christmas tree brighter than anything else in the house. As he led us on, John paused for half a second in front of a prominently placed, professionally lit two-foot-tall Egyptian statuette. In his only reference to the apartment's extraordinary appointments, he turned his head slightly and said, "Original paint."

I saw that ancient statue again in the Metropolitan Museum about three years after John's mother passed away and her apartment had been sold (to a man who told John that he was "going to fix the place up and give it some class"). The little Egyptian fellow sat at the entrance to the Temple of Dendur, with a plaque describing it as 4,500 years old. As I passed, I nodded my head and casually informed an onlooker, "Original paint."

The apartment was grand but unmistakably a home, a place where a family lived. For me, the decor had an emotional impact more than a visual one—it felt strong and timeless. Ancient Roman busts stood beside beautifully crafted ceremonial weapons. Paintings, old-looking and probably famous but unrecognized by me, covered the walls. The library was filled with books, both classic and contemporary, many of them obviously read and reread. Everything was beautiful in a quiet, serious way. Even a brash, preppy punk out of New Jersey couldn't help but be moved by the sheer *quality* of it all.

Walking back toward John's room, my sister and I paused in front of two of the most amazing collages I've ever seen. Mrs. Onassis had filled several four-by-six-foot frames with family pictures from over the years. I distinctly remember a picture of young Knucksy, as I'd begun to call John, sitting on the outsize water-level afterdeck of a converted luxury freighter. There was a Greek island in the background and he was preparing to water-ski. A luxury freighter that you could ski off! The collages were impressive and eerie at the same time. Even with my limited knowledge of Kennedy family history, I thought these pictures were remarkable. They depicted a world that was so much larger than life, and yet the casual snapshot images were just like the pictures my mother took, a record of family moments. Mrs. Onassis's first job had been as a photographer for a Washington paper, and she was clearly fascinated by printed images. She continued to add pictures to her beautiful collages right up until her death, creating a joyful pastiche on the walls of each of her homes. The pictures were all of poignant moments and happy days and, interestingly, all were taken after 1963.

John's room was just past the family picture wall on the left, off the hallway. At first glance it looked like a normal college guy's room, except for the closet. At home I had a closet with some clothes and maybe a football in it. John had a storeroom of industrial-grade adventure equipment. It was like James Bond's closet as appointed by Q, with scuba tanks and boardsailing keels and underwater jet packs and Arctic tents. Sure enough, there was a football in there, except that it was signed by Joe Namath and all the Jets and was bolted to a wooden stand. The only reference to John's dad was a large frame containing a small portrait and signature of each U.S. President up to and including his father. The frame had one of John Kennedy's actual pens embedded in it. I remember noticing that he had no posters of sports figures or rock stars pinned, stapled, or taped to his walls and that his model collection consisted of a highly detailed, fully rigged wooden ship, the USS *Constitution*, that was too big to fit in a bottle and so took up the entire top of his bureau. Despite the fact that this had been his room for close to fifteen years, it didn't seem to have his signature on it. I figured his mother ran a tight ship. Also, he'd spent his high-school years, the time when most teenagers mutiny, out of the house at Andover.

We were hanging out in John's room, my sister and I listening to his continuing overview of his adventure toys, when Mrs. Onassis called for us to come eat. We went out to the dining room, where a spread of gingerbread cookies, ice cream, and milk was laid out on the table. I remember thinking, "Hooray for Christmas!" as Mrs. Onassis got us back in the holiday mood, regaling us with tales of Christmases past. I barely recall snippets of a story of her father and his good humor over a fallen Christmas tree, but I know that she was more animated than I ever saw her again. Though she was about fifty years old at the time, her legendary beauty was not lost on me. She had a broad, symmetrical face with strong features, especially her dark, seductively shaped eyes. It was a refined face, elegant but not delicate or fragile-looking. Slim and with an athletic build, she moved with incredible grace. Every movement was smooth, like a ballerina. Really, though, and I'm not the first to say this, it was her voice that was most extraordinary. She talked in a kind of whisper, low and breathy and compelling, all the while focusing intently on the person she was speaking to.

That was the only time I ever heard Mrs. Onassis speak of her-

Two

AT BROWN

BACK AT SCHOOL, second semester, it was time to choose a place to live for the following year. One rainy Providence Sunday (a trend—it rains a lot up there), John came over to my room to visit. We were talking about our recruiting experiences at the various fraternities, just hanging out, when John interrupted me, asking, very fast, "Whatshouldwedoaboutroomingnextyear?"

I knew what I wanted to do. Helping him through his awkward moment, I responded, "I'd been thinking we'd live together at Phi Psi, with the rest of the guys."

He said, "Sounds good to me."

Although Phi Psi had once been a real fraternity, it had dropped its national affiliation some years back and now operated more like a high-spirited social club. Set in a redbrick building on Wriston, the club consisted of dormlike rooms, each housing two students, a TV room on the main floor, and a bar in the basement. The furniture was from the 1960s, sturdy and ugly like Naugahyde ought to be. Neither John nor I had much interest in Greek society living,

but sophomores were encouraged to live on campus, and joining a fraternity was the only way to keep a large group of friends together. We'd assembled a sizable crew by then. There was John Hare, aka the California Kid, the number one singles player on the Brown tennis team and actually from Illinois; the yellow-eyed Billy Way; Rick Moseley, Brown's starting soccer goalie and a Sean Connery look-alike out of New Hampshire; Tom Haslett, a lacrosse player from the "still British" part of Massachusetts; Mark Rafael, a talented actor; and Gary Weiss, brainy, intense, and another soccer goalie. We'd met the upperclassmen who lived there, and they seemed a reasonable group. So a bunch of us pledged Phi Psi.

I can't remember the name of Brown's admissions director at the time, but he deserves credit for populating the school with an unlikely assortment of students. Many of us were not the typical top-achieving students out of our high schools. Instead, Brown took genuine risks—accepting kids with varied interests, mandating few required courses, and making grades optional—that let individualistic students find their own way. If there was a lot of academic pressure, I missed it. (Of course, I missed quite a few classes as well, so I may not be the best judge.) We weren't particularly political, preferring a good time to a good cause. And 1979 was an easy time to be in college—AIDS was not even named yet, the drinking age was eighteen, and crack, heroin, and Ecstasy were unheard-of on campus. Cocktails and pot smoking satisfied most desires for rebellious experimentation.

John had created a fairly normal life on campus in very little time. Kids who didn't know him well might tell their friends they had John Kennedy in their history class, but most of his days were no different from anyone else's. Then he'd leave for the weekend and someone would see him on television that night, campaigning

for his uncle Teddy or delivering an address at the Kennedy Center in Washington. He rarely mentioned his public appearances to his friends. It was as though he deliberately split himself in two.

Off campus, John remained an object of curiosity. Usually, though not always, the attention he received from strangers was innocent, laced with affection for his father, which John appreciated. Still, it *was* a little nutty to walk down the street and see people stop in their tracks and stare or shout to him, "Hi, John!" I often jokingly asked autograph seekers if they didn't want my autograph as well. "Who are you?" they'd reply. To which John would respond, with reverence, "Why, that's Rob Littell." We made a joke out of it. And I'd learned to enjoy the flash and dazzle of his public life. It was a great show.

By the middle of freshman year, John and I had more or less found our footing, except where women were concerned. I was falling fast for Frannie, while John was in that classic transitional phase between high school and college when you realize that your high-school sweetheart is just that. John's girlfriend at Andover was Jennifer Christian, a natural beauty and emotionally mature girl who was, and is, a salt-of-the-earth type. College presented too many obstacles to keep their long-distance flame burning, but they remained friendly over the years, and John kept a place in his heart for her. I spent only a little time with Jenny, first in 1979 and then again briefly at John's funeral in 1999, but it was clear that John loved her and that they'd had a sophisticated, empathetic relationship. While at eighteen I was barely at the subject-verb-predicate stage of dating, John had already sought and found some depth in his relationships. And he was lucky, or maybe clever, in that the women he went out with were remarkable. Smart, beautiful, and savvy, they all challenged him in some way or other. At that moment, however, I was the one with a girlfriend. This imbalance didn't come between us, though, because John liked Frannie. And more important, he wanted to be in a relationship himself.

A stunning blonde from Southern California was the first Brown student to capture John's attention, around Christmas. As far as I know, she was also the first and only woman to reject him. They never got that close—it was more an elongated fling than a relationship. But they saw each other enough so that when she wanted out, a breakup was called for. She told John the truth, that she'd met someone else. But she left out one little detail, which John heard later through the grapevine—the "other person" was a woman. I barely knew her and don't know if her rumored foray to the other side of the sexual fence was permanent. But I still chuckle at the image of John sitting on his university-issue dorm-room twin bed, head down in confusion, hands wrung in his lap, asking himself, "Did *I* do that?"

Momentarily confounded by love, John did what men have done for ages—he sought solace in sports. He found some first-generation protogym complex in Swansea, Massachusetts, that had a couple of racquetball courts. (For some reason, probably related to his aversion to elitism, he loved racquetball as much as he disliked squash.) I liked a good game of anything, so John and I began a twenty-year career of playing a game we proudly called "stupid ball" because the Ivy League crowd looked down on it. Over that extended time span, we never really improved our skills much. The point was just to leap around and yell and abuse each other and sweat and suffer and lose and win and sweat some more.

I should probably note that I won the first 237 matches. It was years before the playing field leveled, and then it wasn't because I'd lost a step but because John, in his determined way, had become a better athlete. Most people either are born good athletes or don't play sports. John took a tougher route. He was pretty clumsy when I met him, though he had the body of an NFL quarterback. He'd take his shirt off and you'd picture cheering crowds and trophies in his past. Then you'd notice that he could barely walk down the stairs. He dropped more passes and stumbled over more pebbles than anyone I know. Partly it was a psychological thing: As a game, any game, would progress, John would become distracted. He'd realize he was losing his focus, try to compensate, and lose his grip even more. There's an art to closing a match, and it eluded John for years. As a result, I found it ridiculously easy to mess with his mind. I didn't even need to make a good shot. Rather, I'd interject a comment at a critical moment—for instance, when his 9–4 lead had slipped to 9–8 and we were both winded. If I said politely, "We could finish tomorrow if you want," I'd win, 15–9. Simple as that.

Though he wasn't a star athlete, John loved sports and arrived at Brown determined to play *something*. He was what I call athletic scrap. Most kids who excel at a particular sport in high school get to college already knowing the coaches and whether they have a shot at the team. For would-be athletes who arrive without having played a sport at all, there are two paths to intercollegiate play, at least in the Ivy League. First, during orientation week, the veteran crew jocks—that is, the rowers—canvass the school cafeterias looking for prime-grade beef. Because so few high schools have crew teams, it's up to the college teams to find big unspoken-for athletes who love running and pain. Somehow they manage to do it each and every year, staffing the boats with young men and women who look as though they've stepped out of an Abercrombie & Fitch billboard.

If you remain an unclaimed athlete after the crew team has finished, there's still hope. The rugby players are the next to visit the cafeterias, looking for would-be teammates. Ruggers are a different breed, the Oscar to crew's Felix, as wild at heart as the rowers are disciplined. They got John, who ended up a proud Brown rugger. They played miles outside of Providence, since Brown had no field space, so I caught only one game. And John was great—afterward, recounting limericks at the bar. He drank like Jiminy Cricket relative to the average rugby hulk. So, as possibly the worst drinker in Irish history, he compensated with hilarious bar tales and a superior Irish brogue.

He also entertained his teammates with his driving skills, using my car on occasion. I first learned of John's off-road skills from a high-school mate who was attending Princeton. He called one day to ask if I'd been at Princeton the week before. He'd seen my car, driven by a woolly-haired fellow, doing doughnuts on one of the campus greens. I revoked John's driving privileges, immediately and forever, in theory.

Though John's rugby career didn't take him far, there was one sport he excelled at long before he reached college—skiing. He was an incredible alpine skier. In the moguls, in the crud, wherever, he skied with total control and enormous skill. He was beautiful to watch. Of course, he and I battled endlessly, with words and with skis, over who was the better skier. Given that I'm the last one standing, so to speak, I'm claiming victory. John was also a great water-skier, probably the best I've ever seen. And by the time he died, he was as good a football player as any of us who challenged him in Central Park. What had changed most by then was his mind. Not only did he keep himself in great shape while the rest of us moved to the couch, but he had learned to hold his focus in the crunch. Typically, he just kept at it, getting better and better as time went by.

That was John's standard, stealthy shtick—to get better and better at whatever he set his mind to. "Stealthy" because he always maintained an outward cool as he deliberately moved toward mastering something. He had a keen sense of his own weaknesses, maybe because his father had been so accomplished at such a young age. I think he also felt the need to earn, by effort and real accomplishment, the privilege and praise he'd received since birth.

If he'd lived, I'm sure John would have become President of the United States. It wasn't something he talked about in the early years of our friendship, though it seemed perfectly logical to me even then. We joked about it a lot. The first time John ever addressed the issue directly was in 1988. We were at his mom's house, watching the 1988 Republican National Convention on TV. Ronald Reagan's "last ride" movie was playing, and we both had tears in our eyes. As Reagan trotted off into the sunset on his horse, John said, "A guy could learn a lot from that man."

He said it somewhat guardedly, so I pressed him. "Yeah, he sure can ride a horse."

John grinned at me and said, "You've said it yourself, the man can communicate like no one else. Combine that with a working brain and who knows."

I remember that I looked right at him, hard, and said, "It sounds like you know."

John screwed up his face, as though it took some effort to finish the conversation, and replied, "Gotta go home someday, right?"

Surprised at his frankness, though not at his meaning, I laughed and demanded, "Where am I gonna live?"

John snorted and said, "Bangladesh, of course. I can think of no better representative for our nation. And you've always wanted to be an ambassador!"

And he winked. I know it sounds corny, but he did.

Never able to resist an opening, I asked, "Something in your eye?"

He ended with "Nothing at all, Richard. Or can I call you Dick?"

All future discussions on this subject were typically cryptic, but John's intent was clear. And he never forgot to reference my service in Bangladesh.

Three

FRATERNITÉ

———

I'M REASONABLY SURE I got into Brown because I'd been an all-star lacrosse player in high school. I had good SAT scores and I'd been an honor student at Lawrenceville. But high-profile internships, community service, a brilliant essay—I didn't have those. What I did have was a nod from the lacrosse coach, Cliff Stevenson. Cliff was a small man who wore wrinkled clothes and made apparently random roster decisions. He was a master of the Yogi Berra–type remark, as in, "Half of ya over here, half of ya over there, and the rest come with me." Or, at halftime of an important game, "You know what we gotta do? We gotta score more goals than they do. Because, by golly, then we'll win!" I'd been invited to a recruiting weekend at Brown after the assistant coach, Dom Starsia, watched one of my high-school games. As I recall the scene, I was standing outside the Ratty, Brown's main dining hall, getting ready to drive home. Cliff came over and fixed me with his crazy baby-blue eyes. With a voice that was pure James Cagney, he asked the critical question: "If you get into Brown, will you come?"

———

I knew how it worked: I said yes and he made it so. The Ivy League may not have athletic scholarships, but coaches have a couple of spots on reserve at Admissions. And the opportunity was not wasted on me. I played four solid years of award-winning varsity lacrosse and graduated with a political science degree to boot. Admittedly, academics were not high on my list of priorities. In fact, I'm planning on going back to school someday so I can avail myself of all the glorious education I missed. It's possible that education is wasted on the young, but love and sports and play are not, and I was intently engaged in all three.

In contrast, John came to school with clear academic goals. He had a serious streak that made studying feel right, and a genuine curiosity about the subjects he was taking. He was also under considerable pressure to do well, both from his family and from the tabloids, which chronicled his every success and failure. Sometimes it seemed as though everyone had a stake in John's progress. One of the most irritating was a professor who took it upon himself to "mentor" John his sophomore year. Most likely he was thinking ahead to the John F. Kennedy Jr. School of Politics at Brown and wanted John to produce some seminal work for publication. Or maybe he'd been asked by the university to make sure its most famous student did well. Whatever the reason, the worried and worrying man called our room constantly. I considered his phone calls harassment, but John, typically, shrugged it off.

I guess he was too smitten to notice. Despite the less-than-romantic setting that was Phi Psi, John had fallen in love with sweet Sally Munro. She was (and is) a smart, down-to-earth woman from Marblehead, Massachusetts, who physically resembled John's sister and spoke her mind without guile. For John, her honesty and straightforward manner were like a breath of fresh air.

He never really liked dating and the single life, preferring the intensity of a serious relationship, and he and Sally grew close quickly. She was a big influence in his life. It was Sally who suggested to John that people tried hard, sometimes too hard, to be their best when they were around him. She was right, but John hadn't thought about it before. And it bothered him. He mentioned it to me more than once. It meant that people were uncomfortable around him. John, of course, tried to correct the situation by working to put people at ease. Which I figure just made them try harder, but John was an optimist.

Despite John's academic intentions, Phi Psi was no place for the studious. In fact, my head hurts just thinking about our year there. We were given a room, number 201, on the second floor, just to the right of the frat's big stairs leading up from the front hall. The first thing we did was construct two sleeping lofts to free up space for our desks. Next we decorated, which consisted of putting a tiger cub in our window. This wasn't a plushy F.A.O. Schwarz escapee, either. It was a real stuffed tiger cub. I don't recall where John got the tiger, though he was too much of an animal lover to have killed it. In any case, political correctness hadn't been invented yet, so we placed the stuffed animal in the window for passersby to enjoy.

Once our lofts were built, John and I discovered that we had some territorial issues. Each morning, John would leap out of bed and land on an old green couch that my mother had given me. After a few weeks of this Tarzan-like behavior, the couch began to rip. So every morning I was forced to yell at him for not caring about my family's legacy. He'd make his leap and I'd snarl something like "Hey, do you do that at home? Enough on the heirlooms. All right?"

To which he'd reply, "Feck you," in his perfect brogue.

I'd respond, "Do you need a little sign over there? 'No more leaping on the antiques.'"

To which he'd say quietly, "Blow me. This is state government lobby furniture."

John's misuse of my furniture was more than balanced by my own roommate abuses. First and foremost was the Beast. That was the name John gave my closet, as far as I know the only closet on campus to have such a dishonor. Picture the most frightening-looking closet you've ever seen, then think some more. The Beast grew at an astonishing rate, and perhaps because of the organic properties of sweaty socks and balled-up clothes and maybe a crumb or two, over time it took on an animated quality. The whole great smelly mass seemed as if it might just rise up and bite some-one. But I knew where everything was. A little wrestling and—presto!—I could put my hands on socks, shirts, books, the occasional stuffed tiger, and, of course, my schoolwork.

For a time, the Beast kept company with the Smell, a mysteri-ous odor that permeated our room for weeks, gaining wide notori-ety across campus. It was so bad that Frannie and Sally refused to enter the room. Our frat brothers were kinder. They'd come up-stairs, stand as far from the door as possible, and yell in that we had a visitor downstairs.

One day that fall, Mrs. Onassis was one such visitor. She'd come to see John act in a play. One of the brothers yelled into our room that she was there. John sent me down to entertain her while he for-aged for his best shirt. He always treated his mother with the utmost respect, privately as well as publicly, and he usually kept a pressed white shirt around for her visits. I ran downstairs to find Mrs. Onas-

John the freshman as Bonario, a soldier in Ben Jonson's *Volpone.* (Bettmann/Corbis)

sis standing out in the cold on the frat porch. She was looking elegant and a little out of place, as she always did at Brown. She explained that she'd been warned of the smell, and though she didn't want to be rude, she didn't feel the need to go inside. I was embarrassed and tried to apologize, but she just laughed and changed the subject.

Up to that point, rather than solve the problem, John and I had loudly and indignantly blamed each other for causing it. Now that even our mothers were avoiding us, we were forced to take action. Besides, it had become difficult to sleep. We tore apart the room, desperately searching for the source of the odor. As frantic as we were to find the cause, we were just as determined to prove it was the other's fault. So he turned my side of the room upside down and I dismantled his.

I found it (read: it was his fault). Hooray! A mug that had been filled with hot chocolate and whipped cream had fallen and lodged itself, still full, behind John's desk. *Rancid* does not begin to describe the state of its contents. John was crushed, especially since I was supposed to be the pig of the house.

I wasn't able to rest on my victory for long, however, as John launched a counterattack the next weekend. He snuck out in *my* Mazda GLC and drove out to a local farm, where he bought a pig. Thus far I have declined to mention my Phi Psi nickname, for no other reason than that I loathe it. But in the interest of truth, and because John named the little creature after me, I shall admit that I was known as Litpig. The pig, now christened Litpig, was not a cuddly, potbellied Vietnamese pet, but a fast-growing, sty-loving farm animal. And John honestly believed that Litpig would live with us. There was perhaps a twisted logic in bringing Litpig to live with us, but I still don't see it. I banished him from our room. The piglet spent a week in the frat basement in a little tiled corral of sorts, where he had a constant stream of curious human visitors who brought him slop they had secreted back from the Ratty. He pooped prodigiously. The following weekend, with the joke over and the pig's presence known campus-wide, John put him in the passenger seat of my GLC and drove him back to the farm. He dropped little Litpig gently into the pen and left, without even informing the good farmer of his return. I can't say that I missed him.

About a week after saying good-bye to our pet, John came back from lunch one day to find me asleep, resting up for a late lacrosse practice. The weather had gone Providence, which is to say windy, rainy, dark, and cold. John poked me awake to ask if he could borrow my car. Marvel Gym, where we practiced, was about two miles away from our room, so I said no and rolled over.

Our little cube-shaped Sony Dream Machine alarm went off an hour later and I got up to go to practice. Oddly, John was sitting silently on the couch. I assumed he was still pouting and had sat there the whole time in an effort to make me feel bad about not lending him the car. I ignored him.

As I was fishing around in my top dresser drawer for the car keys, John spoke. He said softly, "I crashed it."

Without turning around, I responded, "No, you didn't."

He spoke again, louder now, and unable to keep the laughter out of his voice: "I can't change this. . . . I crashed it."

And then, as if delivering the good news, he added, "I don't think it's totaled, though."

At which point I turned around and made the eight-foot leap across the room to pound him. But I had to hurry, since I had a two-mile run through the freezing rain ahead of me. I arrived in time to get yelled at by the coach and do a few extra laps on John's account.

The car spent four months in downtown Providence, a town with extraordinary family values, as in La Cosa Nostra. The mechanic milked the insurance company for two thousand dollars in storage alone. They'd still be "working" on it if I hadn't instituted a weekly policy of telephoning the garage, inquiring politely as to the status of my car, and then raging uncontrollably into the phone. Twice the proprietor insisted that the car was done and I could come pick it up. Ten minutes later I'd be down there and the same guy would tell me, with a perfectly straight face, that the car was not ready.

The GLC finally made it back about the end of the calendar year. I'd had it for just a few weeks when John requisitioned it for a motorcade honoring the leaders of Sierra Leone. Maurice Tempelsman, Mrs. Onassis's longtime companion and the head of a diamond concern, was entertaining President Siaka Stevens of Sierra Leone, known as the Pa, by giving him a tour of scenic Newport, Rhode Island. There weren't enough official vehicles available for the trip from the Providence airport to Newport. John, with my permission this time, gave the car to a cabinet minister so he could be driven around Rhode Island by his bodyguards. The minister informed John at the end of the weekend that he had learned a lot about American culture—by way of Big Mac boxes, Big Gulp cups, six-pack wraps, and a few textbooks—from my car.

———

One of Phi Psi's attractions was its barroom. With a full complement of taps and refrigeration, the horseshoe-shaped bar usually had visitors seven days a week. A historical mural of the frat's most notorious members covered the walls, lending a comforting sense of continuity. For us sophomores, the thrill of drinking unlimited beer hadn't yet worn off and we gathered in the bar each night until the wee hours. One of our favorite activities was to hold the pinball machine up in the air—it took four of us—so that the player working the buttons could score a new record. We were extremely happy down there, bound to one another by simple camaraderie and the spirit of Augustus Busch.

This same bar was the setting for our fraternity initiation. Although Phi Psi was no longer a chapter of the national organization, it still retained the rituals of a frat house. Everyone who had pledged the year before had behaved well enough to survive the early-fall vetting period. We were ready for initiation night, which fell on a Tuesday. The evening began with the upperclassmen locking us into the bar along with a full keg of beer, half a dozen bottles of cheap tequila, and two bongs. The bongs were for the ounce of weed that was pinned to the bulletin board. We were instructed to finish everything and prepare for the worst. It took about an hour. John then went to man the barricades against the upperclassmen, who were massing outside, eager to take us to our fate.

Phi Psi's de facto spokesman, known to all as the Rabbi, finally made his way in and announced that it was time. Tommy Haslett was up first, he told us. Tommy and John promptly shed a thousand years of collective fine breeding and jumped him, neutralizing the unfortunate envoy and dragging him to the back of the bar. The Rabbi negotiated his release smoothly, as spokesmen do, and was set free. Two larger men then came in for Tom and ended up captive at the back of the bar as well. Nothing happened for about ten minutes. We thought they'd given up when Steve Venditti, a human redwood, came through the door. And Tom went out, in part because of Steve's thigh size but also because we'd started to scare ourselves in there. One by one, we were led from the bar to what turned out to be an entirely reasonable hazing. We were paddled, made to eat a goldfish, and commanded to pick up an olive with our butt cheeks. Amazingly, none of us had a hangover the next day, the alcohol having burned off in a blaze of adrenaline and male bonding.

———

John invited several of his friends to his mother's annual Christmas party in New York that year. I arrived in a yellow cab and, to my surprise, found a gauntlet of photographers flanking the awning of 1040. Even more surprising, they were taking pictures of *me.* I felt sort of out of body—silly and offended and cool, all at the same time. Silly because I wasn't famous and there was no reason to photograph me. Offended because I hadn't given anyone permission to take my picture. And cool because the flashbulbs and the shouting ("Over here! Can you look this way? Merry Christmas! Are you a friend of John's or Caroline's?") sent a surge of adrenaline through me. Upon reaching the newly appreciated privacy of the lobby, I asked the doorman, "Why'd they take a picture of me?"

The gentleman responded with a wisdom gained from years of observation: "Hey, ya never know."

The party was a glamorous affair, with lots of authors and artists among the guests. I recall discussing aircraft carriers with Tom Wolfe (I had read *Mauve Gloves and Madmen,* in which he called them "heaving skillets"), listening to George Plimpton (I *tried* to talk), and laughing with Caroline's costume-designer friend, William Ivey Long. Mrs. Onassis had the aura of a movie star but a warm and perpetually curious air about her, so the party was filled with talented, interesting people. It was fun and exhilarating and much livelier than I'd expected. Although I rarely worried about my rough edges in social situations, I remember mentally thanking my mother that night for whatever etiquette she'd taught me. I also recall checking my hair every nine minutes or so.

After the party ended, John and I went out to Tramps, a jazz bar downtown. There I had my second encounter with the paparazzi. John usually kept his cool in front of the lens, but on this night he was a little spooked. Or maybe being chased by a shouting mob didn't jibe with his sense of Christmas cheer. I didn't know what was happening at first. I'd walked ahead to get the car while John chatted by the door with some people he knew. All of a sudden he came running up to the car, yelling, "Littell, Littell, let's go! They're coming!" Like I was his old Secret Service bodyguard or something.

I've never really liked being called by my last name, either, so instead of flooring it, I crossed my arms and stated, "My name is Rob and I am fine."

John started to laugh. I did, too, a second later. This would become a long-standing joke between us. Whenever John caught me whining, he'd say, "Hey, 'My Name Is Rob and I Am Fine,' is everything okay?" Which usually quieted me down.

Outside of Tramps, the photographers were closing in and we pulled away from the curb in a peal of tires and laughter just as the flashes started to pop. John breathed out, "They sure are a pain in the arse sometimes." (John rarely swore, even when it sounded funny *not* to.)

I snorted that *sometimes* was the key word. He knew what I meant and nodded his head. John was aware of his status as America's boy king. He enjoyed the benefits and had adapted to the cost. His desirability to the tabloids was tied to tragedy, of course, but also to many good things: his fine looks, his charm, his wealth, and his fascinating family. I use a tax analogy with regard to John's sense of obligation: If you have to write a huge check to the U.S. Treasury, it's because you made an enormous amount of money that year. It's no fun to write the check, but it's a lot better than not having made a penny. Or as Larry Ellison says about being a mega-billionaire: "I highly recommend it."

John knew all this, though he had mixed feelings about the paparazzi. He understood that the photographers were just doing their job, but he didn't enjoy being staked out. Every once in a while, he'd lose patience with all the bushes that sprouted feet and camera lenses—say, when we were tossing around a football in the park—and enlist my help. I'd walk up to the offending shrub and say something like "Are you trying to take a picture of *him?* Just come on out and do it, then. Take your picture of the hunk and then do me a favor, will ya? Hit the road."

The photographer would, without exception, mutter, "Sorry," and start walking the other way, camera in the bag.

Overall, they were pretty gentle with him, and he was equally magnanimous with them. The truth is that the press was one of the few constants in John's life. The media had essentially adopted him when he was three, the solemn child saluting his dad's funeral caisson. The attention of the press was like having a friendly dog in the neighborhood. He knew the dog well, knew how to stroke it and make it happy. In return, the dog lavished him with attention and affection. Sure, the papers ran headlines like THE HUNK FLUNKS and pictures of lovers' quarrels, but it was almost always good-natured. When he started *George,* he actually joined their ranks. I'd be willing to bet that if I hadn't been looking that night at Tramps, John would have turned around in his seat and good-naturedly offered them his better side.

———

Back at Brown for second semester, we woke one Sunday to an unseasonably warm, sunny February day. The entire campus came alive, the long winter's gloom momentarily displaced by a rush of spring energy. John and I added to the celebratory mood by placing his stereo speakers out our windows, which faced a church across the street. We cranked the volume to about 9.85, which on John's stereo meant that we were loosening the old cobblestones under the asphalt. The first B-52's album was on the turntable when John Hare came by and asked if we wanted to go to lunch. We did, and walked the twenty yards to the Ratty, where I ate my daily allotment of Premium crackers and white rice—my diet for the year—and John wolfed down his usual four helpings of everything. We were there about half an hour. As we headed back down the dining-hall steps, we heard a terrible, weird sound, possibly coming from our room. It was. The album we'd been playing had a scratch, right at the end of "Rock Lobster." We ran up the stairs to fix it. Two men in dark morning suits were pounding hard on our door. John stepped forward and asked what they wanted. The larger guy was too angry to articulate actual words. He spit out some unintelligible syllables. The smaller fellow stepped in, speaking loudly over the din. I heard just a few key words: "Assholes . . . playing party music . . . it's my grandmother's funeral."

John and I froze. Grandmother? Funeral? 9.85? Holy shit, we *were* assholes! John ever so smoothly stated that he had a key to this room, implying that he was not actually its resident but a hall monitor of sorts. He opened the door and, after letting me slip in, blocked the way. He told the gentlemen, in almost military fashion, "This problem will be addressed immediately. And I'll personally make sure it doesn't happen again. Is there anything more I can do than offer our deepest apology?"

What could they say? John continued, suggesting that he go out to apologize to whoever else might appreciate it. The two men, who were livid a minute before, now backed out of our alcove and down the stairs, actually *apologizing* for their intrusion. It wasn't that they recognized John; they'd just been treated the right way. He could be smooth. We laughed nervously for a few seconds, but we felt bad.

John was deeply immersed in the theater arts program at Brown by then. Most kids who grow up in famous families understand the difference between private self and public persona before they learn to read. So it was only logical that John would love the stage, a place where you can assume another identity completely. He was good, despite the enormous task of making his audience forget they were watching John Kennedy Jr. I've heard people say that John turned away from acting because his mother disapproved. It's true that he didn't seriously pursue acting after college, but that's true for lots of people. The only thing his mother ever said to me about the subject was that she loved watching him act. It was on the porch at Phi Psi, that day when she wouldn't venture near the Smell. She told me that John's acting "brings me the most joy." Which is hardly a reprimand.

Soon enough, springtime arrived in earnest, and just as the flowers began to peek from their beds, the loonies began to come out of the woodwork. We'd actually received hints as to what was coming, though we didn't put it all together. Twice that winter John had gotten elaborate collages in the mail, carefully constructed works filled with pictures of a cute-looking strawberry-blond woman going about her life. There were pictures of her with her parents, at the beach, driving her car, etc. Strangely, the collages also had cut-out pictures of John glued onto them. He had, by virtue of scissors and glue, been hanging out with this woman her whole life. I recall thinking they were kind of sweet.

That was, until the sender blew into our room one lovely Wednesday afternoon near the end of the school year. She had a pink suitcase with her and a stack of collages. John wasn't around just then, but she didn't seem threatening, so I sat down on the couch with her. I listened, silent and shocked, as she went over each doctored picture of her and John, explaining the situation and the good times they'd had together. I'd managed to move several inches away when John came through the door. Jumping up, I introduced them. John looked at me as if I were the loon and we stepped outside our door, politely telling the waif we'd be right back. John asked, "Who the *hell* is that?"

I replied that I was not in charge of his fan club. But in fact we were both a little dismayed. We agreed that he'd get campus security while I stayed with our new friend, Miss Crazy. A long fifteen minutes later the security guards arrived and politely guided her out of the room and on her way home. Or so we thought. They'd actually taken her down to the local Bonanza bus station. It took her and her gear about four hours to get back to our room. We weren't there, but since we never locked our door, she had no problem getting back in. I returned from lacrosse practice about six o'clock and ran upstairs to get my ID for dinner. I knew something was up when I stumbled over my clothes, which were neatly stacked in piles on the landing. It turned out that our visitor had removed all my possessions from the room and rearranged them on the frat stairs. Entering the room, I asked the young lady, who by now had showered and was in her little-girl pajamas, what she was doing. She said, while looking at me as if I were crazy—the second time I'd received that look that day—that *she* was John's roommate now. I backed out of the room in fear, retreating to the TV lounge to await John's return. He arrived shortly and we called security again. They came back, apologized, and retrieved her, but not before making her put my stuff back. Security assured us we wouldn't see her again. Until the next morning, it turned out. We'd locked our door that night, thankfully, so she wasn't able to barge right in. Instead, she pounded on the door for a good five minutes just after dawn. We hid under our covers, hoping she'd just go away. Instead, she went downstairs to the TV room, where she bided her time watching television with a few curious night owls.

This time, the security guards threw their hands up and told us they were going to take our guest to the police. We probably should have let them do so, but John was upset at the thought of this poor, confused person getting hauled away by the black-booted gendarmes who patrolled Providence at the time. After some discussion, we asked the guards to leave her to us, which they did.

We in turn called John Wentworth. Wenty was a friend of John's and an enigmatic artist who'd just completed an art project downtown involving fifty live rats. Perhaps there was a fit. At any rate, we figured he'd know how to handle the situation. John got him on the phone and explained what was up. Wenty came right over. Wenty, an attractive and charming guy, and the young woman got along immediately. He suggested they get some lunch. Over lunch, he told her he was leaving later in the day to drive to Maine. That must have sounded good to her, because the two of them piled into his old-school VW Bug that afternoon and headed for Camden, Maine, where she stayed when Wenty returned to school. She probably owns an art gallery up there now, specializing in collage.

Did we do the right thing? I don't know. Maybe we should have let the police take her. We were nineteen and new to dealing with stalkers, unsure where our responsibilities began or ended.

We didn't talk about it much afterward, either. There wasn't much to say.

Another weird incident happened that year, one that reminded me that celebrity has a creepy side. One evening Frannie and her roommate, Adrienne Homet (whose mother, by coincidence, worked for Ted Kennedy in Washington, D.C.), came by to visit. John wasn't around. The three of us were sitting there, talking and listening to music, when the phone rang. Adrienne was closest to it, so I motioned for her to pick it up. I assumed it was the friendly local professor checking in on John. Adrienne was on the phone for a while, and Frannie and I went back to talking. All of a sudden Adrienne slammed down the phone and started to cry. With the color draining from her face, she said, "Teddy's been shot. The senator's been shot."

We were shocked. But—and this is awful—it seemed entirely plausible. Frannie asked, "Who was on the phone?" Before Adrienne could answer, John came through the door with a bag of Portuguese rolls for us to munch on. Adrienne, through her tears, haltingly told John what she'd heard on the phone. "John, Teddy's been shot."

John was remarkably calm. He put the bag down and asked Adrienne, "Who did you talk to?"

"It was Joe," she answered, meaning Joe Kennedy, one of John's cousins. "He said it was an emergency, that something had happened to Teddy and I should find you. I said my mother worked for the senator and that if anything had happened to him, I wanted to know." She started crying again.

John looked a little pale, but he was still much calmer than the three of us. He picked up the phone and called another cousin, probably Bobby, though I don't know for sure. He was on the phone for only a minute or two.

"It was a hoax," he said flatly after he put down the phone. "Everyone's fine."

We all sat there silently, not knowing what to say.

This was John's life: a little fun, some Portuguese rolls with the gang, and the occasional mention of assassination. He dealt with it, taking the bad with the good. Always smooth.

Four

GRAND TOURING

OUR PLAN WAS to travel to Europe that summer. John could easily have arranged a trip consisting of state dinners in every capital on the Continent. Instead, he and I chose a more personal path. We decided to visit the countries of our ancestors and to explore these lands at pub level. John's ancestry was famously Irish: His great-great-grandfather Patrick Kennedy arrived in Boston in 1848 from County Wexford. He'd left Ireland to escape the Famine and was part of the first big wave of Irish immigrants to come to America. The Fitzgerald of John's middle name came from his paternal grandmother, Rose, also Irish. And on his mother's side, along with the French Bouviers, there were the Irish Lees. So Ireland was on the itinerary.

England made the cut, too, because my ancestor John Littell came from there in 1642 and settled in Elizabeth, New Jersey. Littell is a French name, and John L. was a Huguenot, his family having fled France to England to escape religious persecution in the late 1500s. But neither John nor I spoke a word of French and we

---

figured it would be more sensible to discover Paris with our girl-friends someday, so France was out. On my mother's side I'm Dutch, so we tossed in Amsterdam for kicks. The trip was John's idea, suggested at the end of our sophomore year. He was going to be in Africa for July on a business/pleasure tour of Maurice's company, Leon Tempelsman & Son. I was surprised to learn that John had never been to Ireland but was more than happy to accompany him to the land of Guinness stout. The only fixed point in the plan was our start: We were to meet in London, at the Ritz on Piccadilly Square, on August 2, 1981, at twelve noon. We left everything else up in the air. So on August 2, after a turbulent flight from New York on Laker Airways (which ceased operations several months later), I marched out of an unusually sunny London day and into the elegant lobby of the Ritz. I was wearing a seersucker suit and white bucks—the Ritz was the home of James Bond, in my mind—and my watch read 11:58 A.M., Greenwich Mean Time. Excited, a little nervous, and punchy from the long trip, I stepped up to the tall mahogany reception desk and asked for Victor Legg, the hotel's venerable head porter and the man Mrs. Onassis had instructed us to seek out. Victor walked over from his head porter station at the left end of the long desk and introduced himself. He had an accent as thick as English toffee and was dressed in green tails with epaulets.

Victor directed me upstairs to the room of Bill Ullman, the man in charge of Maurice Tempelsman's African operations. Bill was between duties and resting up in the company's "suite," a closet-size room that could barely contain the two of us. I'd never met him before, but he was friendly and gentle as he broke the news that John had been delayed in Africa and would be arriving several days late. This was not good news, but Bill cushioned the blow by telling me that Tempelsman & Son had arranged to put

Big-haired John
with the Lost
Cousin (John
and a monkey
grand touring in
1981). (Courtesy
of the author)

me up in the honeymoon suite for the interim. A little stunned by
the change in plans, I thanked Bill and mumbled some sort of offer to pay for the room, but he just laughed. As I did later, realizing
I'd never see the bill. And I shall never again get to order three
Heinekens and a filet mignon from the Ritz at four A.M., either. So
to Maurice, I am much obliged.

John showed up on the fifth morning of my stay, after I'd
nearly worn out my legs hiking around historical London. I was
sound asleep when he clattered through the door, a huge pack on
his back and a fearful look on his face. He managed to get out a
"Hey, man," then stuffed his hand into his trousers and pulled out
what is known in Nigeria as an "arm" of marijuana. Relief flooded
his face. He dumped the large bag of contraband on a table and
explained that it had been awkwardly foisted upon him at the airplane gate in Africa by his guide of the past few weeks. It was
meant as a going-away present. Unable to unload it discreetly before he boarded the plane or to stash it safely in the tiny first-class
cabin, John arrived at London's Heathrow Airport in clear viola-

tion of the law, and in a panic. His plan was to dump the pot in the first garbage can he saw before reaching Customs. That didn't work. An airport representative met him at the gate so John could skip the regular visitors' line and zip through the inside office of the Customs Bureau. This should have been a blessing, but as he walked through the office, a German shepherd lunged at him. Animal-loving John misunderstood and reached out to pet the animal, who ignored his affections and instead began barking excitedly, pointing his nose at John's leg. John realized he'd been busted, at least by the dog. He backed out the exit quickly, choking out a "Th-th-thanks!" as he fled. He was still breathing hard when he reached our room an hour later.

I relieved John of his burden by cramming the bag into the garbage bag of a maid's cart, but not before we'd sampled the troublesome gift. And it continued to be trouble. Somehow, in trying to clear the smoke from our room, we managed to break a window. The maintenance men arrived promptly, waving the haze out of their path and commenting with amusement that we "must be having a lovely afternoon!" And they were right—we were happy chaps, a couple of self-proclaimed knights on a visit to the magic kingdom. That's pretty much how we felt the whole trip, as though we'd found the geography to match our mind-set. We knew how lucky we were to be there, and enjoyed every minute of it. It was a great trip, and one that drew us even closer with every laugh we shared.

John and I left the Ritz the next day in grand fashion. Long live the queen, we were somehow still in the hotel's good graces—probably because we looked so ridiculous. Our plan was to have tea with a relative of mine in the afternoon and then leave for Ireland. Accordingly, we dressed in suits and ties, cleaned our white bucks, and hoisted our large metal-frame packs on our backs. John's back-pack was a tribute to efficient travel, filled with wool hiking socks and a mosquito net and the right balance of warm and cold outer-wear. Everything was neatly rolled up and stowed in true *Survivor* style. My pack contained a pair of black wingtips from Brooks Brothers (white bucks are not appropriate for all occasions), a blue blazer, a tennis racket, a pair of jeans, and a Brown lacrosse T-shirt. I had exactly what I needed for a member-guest weekend at the To-keneke Club in Darien. I wore my blazer pretty much every day of the trip, not to look preppy but because I was freezing.

As we took the elevator down to the lobby that morning, one dapper guest, perfectly accessorized down to his pearl-handled cane and silk bowler, looked us up and down and then again.

"Camping, gentlemen?" he asked wryly.

John and I obliged him with a sheepish laugh and set out for lunch with my ex-stepuncle, who, given my family tree, was a close relation. We took a train to Holyhead in Wales, where we boarded the overnight ferry for Dùn Laoghaire, Ireland. It was a sleepless night, our berth being located in the drunken loony section of the boat. Then we headed by train to Dublin, where we planned to meet up with John's cousin Michael Kennedy and his girlfriend, Vicky Gifford, the daughter of football great and sports commen-tator Frank Gifford. What I didn't know was that we weren't meeting up with them right away. First, John wanted to make full use of our camping equipment. He insisted we establish camp in a churchyard outside of St. Patrick's Cathedral with about a hun-dred other Americans, a mix of young Eurail pass travelers and ag-ing hippies.

I hate camping. John loved it. He was a decorated veteran of such programs as Outward Bound and the National Outdoor

Leadership School and liked nothing so much as sleeping under the stars. He was an accomplished outdoorsman, entirely capable, I'm sure, of living on nuts and berries and fish that he caught with his bare hands. He found the wilderness peaceful, and for as long as I knew him he made a point of escaping the city and reconnecting with the natural world whenever possible.

The Dublin churchyard wasn't wilderness, but John was adamant. Lacking a tent, we unrolled our sleeping bags under a tree, receiving a glare or two for our strange attire. (My blazer in particular, I reckon.) John slept like a baby that night, while I cursed every pebble beneath me, mustering perhaps an hour's sleep. I finally gave up and spent the rest of the night wandering the tent-strewn graveyard, musing as to how far man had come. You know: indoor plumbing, electricity, the mattress.

In what would become a trend, John and I avoided Dublin's famed cultural attractions the next day and chose instead to climb up and slide down a small mountain in a park on the south side of the city, Killiney to be exact. We then met up with Wendy Gallagher, the newlywed wife of an old Kennedy family friend, for dinner at a chic restaurant downtown. My luck was about to turn. Mrs. Gallagher, who was about thirty, tall, big-boned, and as rambunctious as any frat boy I'd ever met, insisted we return home with her that evening to visit her husband, who hadn't been able to make it that day. Home was a hilltop castle in County Wicklow, about forty miles away. Hmmm, what to do—sleep in a graveyard of tents, or a castle? John would probably have chosen the graveyard, but luckily for me, Michael and Vicky were in Wicklow as well. We climbed into Mrs. Gallagher's Rolls-Royce, and she narrated points of interest on our trip, including the so-called Wicklow Wanker, an older fellow who exposed himself to us gleefully as we drove by. I slept that night in my own turret—John got one, too—in a king-size bed with satin sheets and an eiderdown quilt.

Dinner was lavish, held in an ornate dining room much larger than the apartment I've lived in for the past fifteen years. Each course was presented by liveried staff on mirrorlike silver serving trays. After we were done eating, the men—our host Paul Gallagher, John, Michael, and I—retired to the pool room in the basement, really the dungeon. We learned and subsequently played billiards, the sense of competition rising with the night's advance. For refreshment, we had simply to amble over to the wine cellar, formerly a large prisoner's cell, and insert the five-pound, three-hundred-year-old key in the ancient keyhole. The wine casks inside were more than eight feet tall. We stayed down there all night, so deep in the keep that we didn't notice dawn's approach. Michael hit the final shot a little after eight A.M., and we retired to our turrets to sleep.

For half an hour. Just before nine, Paul appeared in each of our rooms, hovering like an apparition and dressed in some sort of traditional hunting attire. He ordered us to assemble in the dining room immediately. We stumbled downstairs to learn that breakfast had already been served and that we were heading out for a quintessential Irish experience: the morning Guinness at a local pub. Hungover and as stiff as old hound dogs, we shuffled out to the courtyard, past the empty silver warmers that had contained what was surely a grand breakfast.

Apparently the morning Guinness was a men-only custom, since the women were left to slumber blissfully. We piled into the Rolls and motored up and down too many hills before finally arriving at the pub, a small building of an architectural style made popular by Tolkien's Hobbits. It was packed. We filed in, sat down, and drank our warm beer slowly. This is what's meant by "nursing a beer." I learned that you can gauge the freshness of a Guinness by drawing your initials in the foamy head. If they remain visible when the beer is finished, it was a fresh brew. The bartender also informed us that a child can live to the age of six on Guinness alone. I wondered later how he knew that. John took an especially long time with his beer, moaning involuntarily before each sip. By the time we'd finished our "breakfast," more than a few of the locals were laughing at us. We climbed unhappily back into the Rolls and roller-coastered home.

John and I stayed at the castle for two nights and three days, then headed back to Dublin, rented a red Opel, and started out for County Galway, where Michael had arranged a pleasant excursion. It felt like a long drive, mainly because Michael couldn't—or wouldn't—shut up. He was very funny, but finally John couldn't take it anymore. He turned to Michael and the two of them proceeded to fight like brothers, punching and yelling at each other for two hours. For you women, I'll explain: They were bonding. It was sweet to see.

County Galway is on the western coast of Ireland and looks exactly like the brochure suggested: green fields strewn with rocks in front of a dramatic, jagged coastline. Michael had arranged for us to stay at the Galway Inn, a low-slung stone complex that had great food and a spectacular view. Our visit, he said, would be free, a gift from the inn to express Ireland's pride in the Kennedy clan. John wouldn't have asked for special treatment, but neither of us could think of a reason to turn it down. We checked in and enjoyed ourselves. We got massages and went horseback riding, drank fine wine and ate big steaks, all without thinking of the cost.

Maybe we overindulged. Or maybe Michael had misunderstood the offer. In any case, when we went to check out after five lovely days of lavish living, we were handed a bill that completely wiped out our funds for the rest of the trip. Being the poorest member of the group, I instinctively started to protest, but John put his hand on my shoulder and squeezed it. He pulled a wad of Irish money from his wallet, compelling me to do the same, and we settled up graciously with the innkeeper. We then asked to use a phone and John called home to request that cash be wired to London. As it was his family that had caused our unexpected cash drain, John insisted on making the first cash call. My turn would come later. John and I then found Michael and accused him of treachery and ruination. He laughed at us.

We said good-bye to Michael and Vicky and drove off on the rest of the planned route, visiting Limerick and Waterford before heading back to Dublin. Rather than seeing "the sites," we drank a pint in every hamlet we passed. It made for a rather depressing journey, actually, because every single person we met wanted to come to the United States. I'm pleased when I read about Ireland's recent renaissance, because it was a country in crisis—beautiful but sad—when we were there.

John was completely anonymous on this leg of the trip, just another American kid with a backpack. One kind lady invited us to tea in her home after watching us play Frisbee in the park. On her mantel were two pictures: one of Jesus Christ and the other of John's father. I almost wanted to tell her who was sitting on her couch, because it would have made her day. But John, generous though he was, would have killed me. I think I said something like "What did you say your name was, son?" as we left her lawn. John dropped his chin and didn't answer. We slept in the same park— named after President Kennedy—that night, but we didn't talk about the name. Maybe John had friends who dealt with the ubiquity of his father's name directly but I wasn't one of them. I assumed that John's father was sacred ground to him and that he'd bring him up if he wanted.

He did bring him up from time to time, referring to him as "my father" (never "my dad"), usually in a serious tone. But not always. When Sotheby's held the Kennedy family yard sale in 1996, John wasn't the least surprised at the high prices his father's things went for. Golf clubs for a million bucks? "Cheap! A bargain!" he snorted proudly. A cigar case for four mil? "We're giving stuff away!" he said despairingly. He never spoke of his father's politics. In the more than twenty years that we were friends, we never once discussed the Bays of Pigs, the Cuban missile crisis, *PT 109,* Marilyn Monroe, or Vietnam, although we discussed politics and history a lot.

I don't mean to suggest that John's father was some kind of monster in the closet, just that John was clearly sensitive about him. And I, being a true-to-type WASP, found it easy to avoid the subject. Besides, what could he say? He never knew his father personally. He was younger than three years old when he lost him. No one remembers things from when they were two. So his "memories" came from pictures, from the recollections of others, from the analyses found in textbooks. He couldn't speak about him intimately, which must have been frustrating. I imagine that any young child who loses a parent has to cope with "secondhand" memories. In John's case, though, his loss surrounded him daily. Whether it was a plaque on some wall or a reference to the airport, John's father's legacy was omnipresent. And his absence was underlined. Though we never talked about his father's assassination, it's such a pervasive cultural reference that it seemed to come up all the time. He didn't flinch. Contrary to the stories I've read, I never saw John leave the room when the Rolling Stones song "Sympathy for the Devil" was playing. Actually, if we were in the car or some other private place, he'd sing out, even yell, the lines:

I shouted out,
Who killed the Kennedys?
When after all
it was you and me.

He never looked at me when he did it. And he didn't laugh. But sing he did. I think he took some sort of solace in the rock 'n' roll glorification—by his beloved Rolling Stones, no less—of his dad.

It didn't help that John's birthday, November 25, was so close to the November 22 date of his father's death. In 1988, the twenty-fifth anniversary of the assassination, John told me that he wished his birthday fell somewhere else on the calendar. He made a similar comment in 1993, on the thirtieth anniversary. We were Rollerblading in Battery Park, planning on hauling up to Central Park for the exercise. John was lagging the first mile, so I asked if he was tired. This was the sort of question that normally got me passed in a cloud of smog. Instead, John told me that the media coverage of his father was "not so easy" emotionally, and that he'd prefer to just go get a beer. We ended up at Puffy's on Hudson Street, where I made an effort to let John vent if he wanted. But we stuck to our usual program, playing tough guys in the face of our past.

The park in County Cork had a bronze-relief sculpture of John F. Kennedy at the entrance, youthful and smiling. I walked by it the next morning, wondering if he'd been responsible for the surprisingly good sleep I'd had. John looked at it as well. I can't even imagine what he was thinking. We left the park and drove directly to Dublin, where we were staying one more night before returning to London. In search of music and some girls to flirt with, we went to a nightspot called the Paris Disco. It had the feel of a high-school dance, with an open bar. The phrase *sexual tension* does not begin to describe the atmosphere. There were maybe forty men in the basement club, lined up in five rows of eight at the bar. When the front line was served, the group of eight, who all seemed to know one another, would rotate to the back of the line. The next row up, as if guided by a metronome, would finish their beers just as they reached the bar. The whole rotation took about fifteen minutes, and it went like clockwork.

John and I got in formation and mastered the rhythm quickly, though John needed two cycles to finish his beer. As we watched, we saw there was another component to the process: Every ten minutes or so, when one of the lads was cockeyed enough to ask a woman to dance, he'd totter across the dance floor, where maybe twenty women were congregated about their own, smaller bar. The other men would look on as if one of their own had died, sometimes leaving their position to retrieve a mate who fell, drunk or perhaps disoriented by the flashing disco ball. John started to help one guy who'd fallen but he was held back by the man's pals, who let their buddy stew on the floor for half a minute before jostling him upright. The women giggled.

"Well," said John as we were leaving, "that helps explain why Grandpa Patrick left."

By the next evening, we were back at the Ritz in London. Sadly, our stay lasted only the ten minutes it took for kind Victor Legg to give us the cash Mrs. Onassis had wired. Victor asked us where we were staying that night. We smiled politely, thanked him for his help, and left. We spent the night snug in our sleeping bags in

Hyde Park, a stone's throw from the honeymoon suite I'd slept in not long before. Our urban campsite was encircled by eight park chairs we'd set up to protect us from the police Land Rovers that roared through the park at night. I missed the room service. John, of course, was perfectly content.

The following day, we were off to the port city of Newcastle, on the southern coast of England, embarking on an overnight ferry to Amsterdam. It was a miserable trip salvaged by the sight of a magnificent tall ship making its way up the Amstel River in the morning. Actually, this was typical of our Grand Tour: We'd get off to a miserable start, not being morning people, and then go on to memorable adventures and hours of hilarity. Our wondrous view this time was the 375-foot *Kruzenstern,* from Russia, which I'd seen at the U.S. Bicentennial celebration in 1976 and would see again with John at the Liberty Centennial in 1986.

On to the Kabul Inn, a youth hostel in the red-light district of Amsterdam. The rooms were huge, filled with enough bunk beds to hold forty people, and the facilities looked exactly like a stadium bathroom. We were awakened in the morning by the sound of the naked Swedish twins giggling in the bunks next to us, but we checked out anyway and found a cozy little inn called the Dam right off the main plaza in the old city. That night we went out to experience Amsterdam's famed red-light district. Our evening began at the famous Milkweg bar and dance club. After witnessing a criminal assault on some musical instruments there, we proceeded up the street, stopping at another Heineken outpost and ordering a round to screw up our courage. Then we headed back to the red-light district to avail ourselves of the reasonably priced talent that preens in the ruby-lit storefront windows. Sadly, my libido was overcome by my guilt, or maybe a lack of *cojones.* But John, who was between serious girlfriends at the time, suffered no such pangs. I felt like a total loser, waiting down the street for John to arrive with tales of a tall, beautiful blonde.

Sticking to our traveling method, we saw very few of the recommended tourist sites in Amsterdam. We did visit the zoo, where I took pictures of large tropical fish. We rented bikes with the idea of touring the city, though within a few blocks of the bike shop we lost interest in touring and hurled ourselves into a fiercely competitive race to an unknown finish line. We literally careened through the city for three straight hours, trading the lead back and forth, attempting to lose the back rider in the alleys. The final lap turned out to be a stretch of road, the Stadhouderskade, that passed right under a large ornate building. I was ahead at the time and noticed a brightly colored poster indicating that we were flying past the Rijksmuseum, one of the finest museums in Europe. We blew by it in seconds. John, focused on regaining the lead, didn't even notice that we were hurtling past the House of Rembrandt. Without slowing, I yelled back, "Hey, that was the Rijksmuseum."

"What?" he barked, the museum three blocks behind us by now.

"That . . . was . . . the . . . Rijksmuseum!" I shouted breathlessly.

At which point, out of energy and apparently finished with our race, we slowed and fell in a heap of metal and flesh. Lunch and a long nap completed the barbarian tour.

We ran out of money again that evening. It was my fault. I was missing Frannie badly and decided to give her a call. I entered the little phone booth embedded in the wall of the hotel lobby and called the States. There was a meter in the booth, a little silver box with maybe ten digits of rotating counters that indicated the cost of the call in guilders. (Guilders, gone now in the wake of the euro, were beautiful banknotes that looked just like play money.)

As I was talking, saying nothing in particular but completely lost in the pleasure of talking to my girlfriend, the meter reached twenty guilders, then stuttered and stopped. I didn't think twice about it. A short while later, a hotel attendant whose face did not reach the window on the door started banging on the booth. He was yelling, in crystal-clear, panicky-sounding English, "One hundred twenty guilder!"

Then moments later, with a higher pitch, "One hundred twenty-five guilder!"

Now, I was in love, so this faceless gentleman had absolutely no effect on me. I just kept talking. What's a guilder, anyway? A moment later John, who'd been fetched by the desperate attendant, burst into the phone booth and ripped the phone out of my hand.

"What are you doing?" he demanded incredulously. But he knew. And it was too late.

My extended love call had left us with just enough money to get back to London, where we could place another cash call home, my uncle acting as the intermediary this time. We stuffed our wardrobes into our backpacks the next morning and headed for England. Which was a bummer, because we'd just scratched the surface of Europe. We'd missed much of what we were supposed to see, the museums and the historic sights, because we were too busy having a ball, enjoying each other's company in these new, fantastical settings. But the date on my return ticket said it was almost time to go home.

English Customs, this time in the coastal city of Brighton, once again proved a problem for John. Two young border guards with big, red-faced heads noticed that his passport was special. "Special" in that it was valid only for entry into South Africa, a formality required by the State Department because of U.S. sanctions against apartheid. John had lost track of his regular passport a few days before, when it was either stolen from his pack at the Kabul (his theory) or lost during our wanderings (my theory). John hadn't worried much about it, because, well, he was John and he also had a superofficial ID in the form of his "special" passport. We figured entering England wouldn't be a problem.

It was a problem, or at least an entertaining diversion for the border guards. The two immediately realized who was standing in front of them, without the requisite documents. Like two cats who'd just cornered a mouse, they began quietly. They mused out loud, looking at John's inadequate papers, "So, you don't have a valid passport and you want to come into England?"

That's what they said. But this, when John and I compared notes later, is what we both heard: "Ahhhh. Mr. Big Swinging American Prince is upstream without a paddle on our watch."

I was already on British soil by now, having been stamped through by the same two blokes moments earlier. When I realized what was happening, I snorted softly. John's interrogators looked up, acknowledged their audience with sly smiles, and returned to their game.

The shorter, stouter one asked John, "Well . . . do you have a plane ticket home?"

His face a little red, John admitted that no, he didn't have a plane ticket. The taller guard then repeated the chorus: "No passport, no ticket home, and you want to come into England."

Short-and-Stout then asked John if he had any money. He did not. Not one dollar or guilder or pound. I had the cash, all three pounds of it. John wisely assumed a humble stance, lowering his head and replying, "No, I have no money. Either." This last was sort of squeaky.

The tall one summarized again, this time in a tone that implied he might just turn John back, leaving him stuck between ports on the English Channel forever.

"Let's get this straight, guv-ner," he said slowly, speaking to John as if he hadn't seen anyone as clearly criminal in a long time. "You have no passport, no ticket, and no money. And you want to come into our country." It was a question, but he didn't say it like a question.

At which point I let loose a loud American-style guffaw.

John didn't look at me, either because he was annoyed or because he was afraid he'd burst out laughing himself. Instead, he raised his head, looked them both in the eye, and mustered a truly sincere "Sorry."

The cats let the mouse go. In fact, having had their fun—as they were entitled—they actually carried John's pack over the line for him. John, as red-cheeked as I ever saw him, kept his eyes on the floor on his ten-foot perp walk across the border.

Our tickets took us through to a London tube station, but we lacked cab fare and so had a long, cold walk to the Ritz. We asked to see the one and only Victor Legg, who lent us five pounds.

You should always repay your debts. Several years later, while making conversation with Mrs. Onassis during the intermission of a play at New York's Public Theater, I suffered the shame of the deadbeat.

"Oh, Rob, did I mention that I saw the good Victor Legg this past month?" Mrs. Onassis asked casually.

Instantly reminded of our irresponsible behavior, I stammered, "Uh-uh-uh . . . n-n-no . . . uh . . . no . . . What a great guy!"

She leaned over, dropping her whisper of a voice a notch softer, and said, "You're all square with him now. He is *truly* a lovely man."

I may as well have baaed like a sheep, but I said, "Yuh, great! Thanks a lot. Sorry. Won't happen again."

She smiled. I felt a little nauseous.

It's probably good she didn't know how we spent the money: on two pints of Guinness and two tickets to *Caddyshack*. When the movie was over, we made camp about half a mile away from our last spot, in a grassy area called St. James's Park. We unfurled our sleeping bags up against a pond to avoid getting run over. I was actually sound asleep, having learned against all odds to sleep in the dirt, when a ferocious barking sound woke me with a jolt. Two lunging, snarling rottweilers, barely restrained on their leashes, were snapping and growling less than a foot from our faces. Their owner, no doubt a good citizen who didn't appreciate the New World trailer park we'd made of the queen's grounds, didn't say a word. He just allowed his two terrifying beasts to snap and growl at us as we lay there, frozen in fear. Then he walked away. When the adrenaline subsided, we fell back asleep. Until a Range Rover drove right up to our feet and a chipper bobby asked, through the 120-decibel public-address system attached to his truck, "Nuf sleep, gentlemen?"

We leaped to our feet, grabbed our stuff, and stumbled away, my seersucker trousers dragging behind my backpack. We made it to the relative comfort of a wooden bench at the park's entrance before collapsing. Only then, eyes open in the light of early morning, did we realize that we had slept right in front of Buckingham Palace.

Given how badly the night had gone, it only made sense that we'd be a little grouchy the next day. We were in the British Museum, attempting to compensate for all the art-and-culture stuff we'd missed, when we started arguing. I don't remember what it was about. All I remember, as did John later, is that John was so distracted that he walked right by a large mirror in the lobby—and didn't look in it. This was a first in my experience. I had never known him to miss a mirror. Still angry over whatever it was we were fighting about, I said loudly, "You missed one!"

He knew exactly what I was talking about. He turned around and stomped out of the museum. I wasn't about to follow. So we lost each other and had no backup plan. We were supposed to stay at the house of my ex-stepuncle that night, a man by the name of Johnny McCarthy. But I'd never given John the address, so he had no idea where to go.

I made my way over to my uncle's for supper, looking forward to a real bed and the cash my mother had wired over. I walked into the living room and there was John, drinking tea and sharing stories with my uncle as if they were old friends. Two points for him. I have no idea how he got there, because I refused to ask. For the next eighteen years, though, whenever a mirror came into view, one of us would shout, "You missed one!"

Am I saying that John was vain? Yup. Can you blame him? The guy was a walking, talking Greek statue. And he knew it. If *People* magazine had ever replaced him as the world's sexiest man, I'd have had to watch him cry.

John also loved clothes. He came by his sense of style naturally, of course, given that Mrs. Onassis was the epitome of chic. And it didn't hurt to get the gifts and discounts that designers and manufacturers give to celebrities. If designers sent me nice clothes and invited me to shop at a discount in their stores, I might look better, too. Actually, I looked better just for knowing John, since he gave me loads of sports stuff he received from Adidas. (I'm still wearing it, even though I'm a Nike man.) He took great pleasure in mocking my rumpled wardrobe, though in fact most of his friends weren't stylish in the least. He would often tug my collar to see what label I was wearing and then laugh at me for having too little taste and paying too much money. Later in life, he had at least fifty suits arranged by slight gradation of color in two closets in his apartment. He'd sometimes thumb through my three, usually dirty, suits with grunts of pity, muttering words like "threadbare" and "dry cleaner." Fashion was one of the few areas where John assumed the role of an elitist. He was a natty dresser with a competitive streak, and because style is a sport where nobody gets hurt, he mercilessly vanquished all around him.

Having added the mirror to our shared repertoire of private jokes, we came to the end of our Grand Tour and made our way back to the States separately. I left my uncle's house a day earlier than John because his passport issues needed ironing out. Mrs. Onassis had invited me to stay at her place when I got back, to wait out John's return so he and I could debrief each other. I slept late the first morning back, jet-lagged but giddy from the whole incredible (at least to me) travel experience. As I wandered out of the bedroom in search of food, I walked by a large study, one of the apartment's fifteen rooms, and saw Mr. Tempelsman working at a big table. A beautiful old gilt desk that looked as if it had snuck out of the Louis XIV collection of the Met across the street stood between two sets of doors that led to a terrace. Mrs. Onassis had her chair facing away from the small television—strange, I thought— that was housed in a cabinet under the bookcases. Bookcases covered the walls, filled with old hardcover books, including several large black portfolios that were Mrs. Onassis's private family anthologies. These leather-bound tomes were part of a tradition started by John F. Kennedy after his brother Joe was killed in World War II. The first volume in the series was titled "As We Remember Joe."

Walking by the study that morning, I said cheerfully, "Morning, Maurice!"

Then stopped, took three steps back to the doorframe, and corrected myself. "I mean, Mr. Tempelsman."

I walked on, hearing him call out warmly, "Maurice is fine. Get some breakfast!"

Maurice had just arrived from Africa that morning and was no doubt eager to reclaim his room, where I'd slept the previous night. The guest room was large and bright during the day, situated on the south side of the apartment. It was not a suite but shared a door with Mrs. Onassis's room. Incorrigibly curious, I'd opened that door, not knowing where it went, and was shocked to find myself looking into Mrs. Onassis's bedroom. Thankfully, she was long gone for the day. Her room was bright and airy, with a dazzling view of Central Park. There was very little furniture and just a few decorative objects. I recall two framed pictures, of John and Caroline as toddlers. The most remarkable thing about the guest room was the closet, home to maybe forty pairs of seemingly identical, well-ironed white slacks. I had found the original source of all Capri pants.

On the way toward the kitchen, I passed two large mirror-backed tables, each covered with jewel-encrusted swords and enameled boxes that looked Ottoman. After Mrs. Onassis died, John kept one of the smaller swords, a highly detailed blade with a ruby-covered dagger attached to the scabbard, on the coffee table at his apartment on North Moore Street. I walked by the French doors in the living room and was momentarily stunned by the vastness of Central Park, which spread out to the north and south of the apartment. The Central Park reservoir, now named after Mrs. Onassis, sparkled in the sun directly in front of the living-room terrace.

In the dining room, I knew, sat the one reference to Mrs. Onassis's role as First Lady, at least the only one I ever saw. It was a big black photo album with an enormous gold presidential seal on it. It sat on top of a concert grand piano. I never looked in it. There, in that house, it looked formidably private and, despite the official seal, utterly personal. It was an inanimate object that somehow felt alive. I felt as though there was a Secret Service agent behind the curtain to guard it.

At last, I made it to the kitchen, where Marta was still wielding her spatula and treated me to breakfast, without Guinness. Marta "Scooby" Squbin entered John's life when she was hired as a governess for him and his sister in 1969. By the time I met her, she more or less ran the household and had a warm, familial relationship with John. Marta had a tough-love way about her that kept all of us in line. I could never get a handle on her accent; I just did what she told me to do. Marta was smart and tough and capable, and she managed to make John's friends feel connected to the family in a way that Mrs. O, because of her fame and her reticence, couldn't, notwithstanding her graciousness. In later years Marta held my kids and fussed over their breakfasts. That morning she fed me close to two pounds of American bacon and a dozen or so 100 percent U.S. English muffins. I stopped chewing only to thank her. John returned the next day and we had lunch before I headed back to my mother's house in Princeton. Despite our high spirits, we admitted to each other that we'd missed a few highlights on our drive-through adventure. In the spirit of friends forever, we took a solemn oath to do the whole trip again someday, with stops at the museums.

College Hill historic district, and John shared it with several friends. The house was inhumanly cold in the winter. Our landlord was a man named Ronnie who lived in Washington, D.C., and was never seen. His mother lived two doors down from us and kept a shrewd eye on her son's property. If one of us accidentally slammed the door, she'd poke her head out of her screened back door and bark, "What's going on?"

My housemates, besides John, were the sweet and beautiful Cordelia "Dee" Richards, John "the Bear" Hare, and Christiane "Kissy" Amanpour. Kissy, the smartest of us all, didn't go to Brown; she commuted to the University of Rhode Island each day. In between, she made sure we didn't all freeze and starve to death. Like a den mother, or maybe a general, she laid down the rules and we followed them. We each had to shop and cook once a week and were charged with specific areas to keep clean. The biggest job at 155 Benefit Street was message-taking, because the phone rang off the hook most of the day. The house ran like a Swiss watch. Dinners were not quite formal but still represented a quantum leap in civility from our frat-house routine. Over good (occasionally great) food, we would engage in dinnertime conversation that was serious and stimulating. I was the sole conservative in the group, a Republican by "accident of birth," as JFK Sr. had once said to explain why he was a Democrat. Thus, I usually ended up as the knuckleheaded "counter" to Kissy's fiercely well-informed "point." I required constant assistance from John, who, while firmly on Kissy's side in nine out of ten debates, acted as the de facto mediator between us. It helped me that John wasn't a traditional liberal. He shared the liberal values of his Democratic family, but his thoughts on how to achieve those ends were at times surprisingly conservative. (Something we moderate Republicans refer to as "practical.")

Ronald Reagan was President at the time, and John and I both admired him. John had also lived too close to the epicenter of political power all his life to see things in terms of pure ideology, or "good guys" and "bad guys." So, to my great relief, he listened to my ideas with an open mind, despite my unpopular party affiliation, and we found that we often agreed, at least in principle.

Of all of us, Kissy went on to the most extraordinary career, becoming one of our era's greatest war correspondents. From what I could see, she began her career of observing and analyzing conflict at a young age. Born in London to a British father and an Iranian mother who was effectively exiled from Iran during the Ayatollah Khomeini's revolution, she grew up knowing the personal dimensions of political conflict in a way that few Americans do. Her academic focus was on global relations and she'd written several brilliant papers arguing, among other things, that we needed female voices in the world's capitals to pull humanity out of its seemingly permanent cycle of violence. I remember sitting painfully cross-legged in front of Kissy's bookcase, studying a long paper she'd written titled "Hawks Versus Doves." My hope was to find some nugget that would let me win at least one friendly argument. But I was destined to lose every time. The only thing I ever convinced her of was my need for extra helpings of her excellent Persian rice dishes, with the bottom layer perfectly crisped.

I had one memorably bad afternoon that fall, which John helped me through with comedic flair. Frannie, who was away that semester studying in Paris, sent me a letter asking why I hadn't written more (actually ever) and wondering where my heart lay. I spilled my remorse to John, saying that my heart felt staked and I could think of nothing to convince her of my lasting affection. John thought for a minute, the lightbulb went on above his head, and he said, "Send her a sock, man. Pull a sock from the Beast and mail it to her." Dirty socks being something of a signature, I guess. Actually, I didn't totally get it, but he had a better way with the ladies than I did, so soon enough a sock (clean, out of respect) was winging its way to Paris in an envelope. Two weeks later, I got a call from my beloved. John had saved my relationship. She's still laughing.

John had done reasonably well at school his sophomore year, spending more time at the library than the rest of us with NCAA commitments. On Benefit Street, however, he became a real scholar. And he did amazingly well, especially if you consider that he really did see some letters backward. Through a combination of hard work and sheer smarts, he mastered his subjects and in celebration lined up all his completed textbooks on the mantel in his bedroom, like trophies. His desk, now appointed with one of the many replica "presidential chairs" he owned over the years, was a tribute to organization. This was important, since he always had a huge load on his plate. John carried the schedule of two people most of his life. He got at least twice as much mail, twice as many phone calls, and three times as much unsolicited advice as the average busy person. There was always something going on, whether it was a Kennedy Library event or a cousin's campaign or a charitable obligation. It was a combination of energy and sense of duty that kept him going, though every once in a while he would be overwhelmed by all that was asked of him. One time, a high school in Alabama formally and very sweetly requested that he be its commencement speaker. Not the type to crassly toss an invitation into the round file, he went into a funk because he couldn't say yes. He missed two lectures that day, sitting at his desk crumpling up letter paper in an attempt to respond. Basically, he couldn't find the other words to accompany the only one—"no"—he had to write.

John was more studious than he let on. Like most kids at school, he wanted to do well without looking to be trying hard. At the time, we scorned "overachievers." There was a general prejudice at Brown in favor of understatement, authenticity, and the superiority of the diamond in the rough. It extended past academics into every aspect of life: We wore wrinkled, who-cares clothes, even the rich kids drove beat-up cars, and very few girls wore makeup. You were either beautiful or you weren't, effortlessly smart or not—effort only compounded the problem. Things changed during the early 1980s, when Brown became a "hot" school and much harder to get into. All of a sudden, seriously accomplished students showed up on campus, along with convertible BMWs and stylish clothes. But we wanted to get by on pure brilliance—and no work. When John's sister, Caroline, referred to him and me once as "underachievers," we were flattered. Except that John wasn't, and could never have been, a slacker, since he felt too strong a sense of obligation to live up to the hopes of others.

I managed to balance sports, social life, and schoolwork better that year than I had before. Meanwhile my roommates were approaching Graduation Day. Like graduates everywhere, they were bombarded with parents and older friends telling them that "college is the best time in your life." What kind of line is that? Who wants to hear that the best part of your life is over? All I'll say is that it was a great time—I hope to better it. Our backyard on Benefit Street was always occupied with people talking, sunning, and barbecuing. It was like a little Malibu Beach community in rainy old Rhode Island. I participated in the fun as if I were graduating, too. I wasn't particularly upset about missing the mortar-and-tassel festivities, mostly because I loved playing lacrosse at Brown and was looking forward to another year. Also, everyone who was leaving was a little worried about what they'd do next.

Graduation Day came. We were exhausted and hungover because we'd hosted a big all-night bash at our house the night before. Putting down our beers at seven-thirty that morning, we'd all showered and changed into clean clothes. The odd transition from night to morning cast the day in a strange haze. The surreal atmosphere—everyone lined up in suits and skirts at the unholy hour of nine A.M., having last slept maybe a week ago—was compounded by a blazing hot sun that appeared from another state to fry the pale seniors in their polyester robes. I don't remember anyone being elated, because we realized that a remarkable time was coming to an end. So we were proud of one another but a little stricken that it was over.

John received a lot of attention that day. There were a bunch of professional photographers in the crowd, taking pictures for the tabloids. Lots of parents were keen on getting a shot of John, too, some even yelling for his attention as he walked by. Out of the blue, a good friend glued himself unnaturally to John's shoulder as the seniors marched up College Hill, obviously determined to be in the news photos. John brought it up later that night, asking me if I'd noticed the strange tactic. He was surprised and maybe a little nervous. John's assimilation at Brown was so complete, his celebrity so compartmentalized, I think we'd all forgotten about the outside world.

The other unexplained thing that happened that day was that our house was raided. Surreptitiously and, I believe, illegally. And as far as I know, I was the only witness. At about eleven A.M. I came

Graduation Day at Brown in 1983. From left: Anthony Radziwill, John's mom, friend Randy Poster in Ray-Bans, and the scholar clutching his diploma. (Bettmann/Corbis)

back down the hill from campus to get some film. There in the backyard were eight to ten Rhode Island state troopers. Not Brown security, not Providence police, but state troopers. They didn't bother to acknowledge me as I entered through the gate, nor did anyone concern himself with that constitutional nicety, a warrant. As I walked up to the house, the senior officer was coming out the back door with a big smile on his face. He barked out, "Let's go." They piled into three unmarked cars and roared off down the hill. I walked into the house, curious as to what I might find, and even more curious as to what the troopers had found. I could not figure out why they had been there. It seemed weird that anyone, let alone the state, would do that. Were they looking for a little international press? Had some neighbor or bitter fellow student called them? Was this the political powers that be in Rhode Island looking to take a swipe at their more glamorous rivals in Massachusetts? That's my theory: some dirty politics in action.

I walked through the house to see if the troopers had rifled through the place. Everything was more or less in the same disorder as we'd left it. There were a few roaches and a bong lying around, which the troopers had left untouched. And since they were laughing on the way out, it didn't seem that it would come to anything. But I felt uneasy, as though the real world was getting closer much too fast.

The day after graduation John threw a huge graduation party for a group of about fifty Brown students in Hyannis Port. I don't remember much more than people sleeping in the emptied pool and in the screening room beneath the grand matriarch Rose's big house. Frannie and I stayed in John's mom's place, which was a bit off to the side and in the back, consistent with Mrs. O's slight estrangement from the local gang. (I was surprised, though, when John ultimately considered unloading the house. By 1996 he had too many properties on his personal Monopoly board. He spoke of the possibility of his oldest pal, Billy Noonan, buying it, though that didn't work out because the house was part of the contiguous family compound.) Leaving Hyannis Port the next day, which was hard because of the great energy we'd generated, a small group of us headed to the Vineyard to continue the never-ending party on Mrs. Onassis's 150-acre slice of Eden. We stayed for days, reluctant to let the party end.

Six

AT HOME IN THE CITY

SCHOOL OVER, JOHN headed back to New York City, a place he loved with all the intensity and complicated emotions that true love entails. He knew New York the way people know their own homes: the quietest place to get the morning sun; the best spot to toss a Frisbee; the places to avoid because the proprietors, like creaking floorboards, would betray his presence to the paparazzi.

Being John, he devised all sorts of games to keep himself amused: racing the bike messengers on his bicycle (dressed in a green gas mask and ski goggles), surfing the wake of the Staten Island ferry in his kayak, playing handball in Spanish Harlem, Rollerblading down potholed Broadway, and most of all, catching football passes in Central Park.

New York City loved John back. He was the city's native son, her royal progeny, protected and accepted, no matter what the situation. I always think of the *New Yorker* cover the week that John's plane crashed: an illustration by Ana Juan of the Statue of Liberty

---

wearing a black veil of mourning. It still makes me teary. I thought of John a lot when the Twin Towers fell, too, wishing he were there to talk to and knowing how much he'd have been hurt by the attack on his home. It was the biggest thing in my adult life that I didn't share with him.

While I was finishing up at Brown, John was bouncing around the city and country and world, living out of a suitcase. He hung with his longtime girlfriend, Sally Munro, and they traveled together to India, where John studied at the University of Delhi. We spoke on the phone occasionally, and I saw him when I went down to visit Frannie, who was now living and working in the city, but mostly we were busy doing our own thing.

After graduating in 1984, with a political science degree tacked to my lacrosse stick, I packed up my car, now a two-seater MGB, and headed toward real life. My eventual destination was New York, but I wasn't in any hurry. My mother was then living with her husband, David Katz, in a big cushy house they'd built on a golf course in Princeton. I got home from school, found a lounge chair by the pool, and hunkered down. I love David, happily still my stepfather many years later, and I knew for sure that there wasn't any better real estate awaiting me in New York. Alas, Mom and David decided to move to California and sold the house. It was probably the only way to get me to leave. I was the last out, going down one side of the circular driveway as the new owners were coming up the other.

But the transition to New York was easy: Frannie was there, and John, along with almost everyone else I'd known at school. John and I decided to get an apartment together and looked at places all over the city, including several downtown, before settling on one on the West Side, a few blocks from Central Park. I don't know why we even bothered to look elsewhere, since John insisted on being near Central Park. I joked that he needed to be near Mummy, especially when he'd go out to get the facials she arranged for him. Probably the original metrosexual, John enjoyed the spa and was never bothered by my mockery. He liked his mother, too, though he didn't really spend a lot of time at 1040. And he knew, as I did, that you're lucky if you get to be a mama's boy. Mrs. Onassis has been portrayed as an overbearing mother. I think that's simplistic. She was strong-willed and opinionated, certainly, and it wouldn't have been any fun to earn her scorn. She went to extraordinary lengths to protect her children and held them to high standards. But she was careful not to overstep her bounds. She let John be John. While she tried to help him avoid mistakes, I don't believed she actively interfered—beyond the standard motherly nagging—in how he lived his life. Besides, she'd shown pretty good judgment over the years where her children were concerned. So she earned her influence. And she was cool—John was unabashedly proud of her.

Our new home was at 309 West Eighty-sixth Street, a two-bedroom, two-bath sublet with alley views that we got through a broker at Feathered Nest, a realty firm. She gave us a little Tiffany obelisk when we moved in, which made us think we'd paid too much. The apartment's owner had moved to Paris to work as a bureau producer for *ABC News*. Somehow we convinced him and the co-op board that we were aspiring monks and they let us move in. It was a renovated prewar building, not fancy but nice. The only problem we encountered was deciding who would get the master bedroom, which was much more luxurious than the other one.

John, the born diplomat, suggested right away that we switch rooms every six months rather than pay different rents, which I suppose might have been awkward.

Our life on Eighty-sixth Street had a different rhythm than at school, what with jobs and all, but we found time to party. I was working at a small brokerage firm, Evans and Company, and John worked quietly for various good causes, essentially taking a working break between his undergraduate education and law school, where he'd decided to go soon after graduating from Brown. The Kennedy family had a longtime interest in special education and John devoted many hours to working on projects that ultimately became serious charitable efforts, including the East Harlem School at Exodus House and Reaching Up. He took a small salary from the New York City Office of Business Development from 1984 through early 1986 and served as the deputy director of the 42nd Street Development Corporation in 1986, working under his mother's good friend Fred Papert. He did some acting for fun during this period. He began to study for the law boards in 1985, with the idea of starting law school in the fall of 1986.

But work was just one priority: It was the mid-eighties and New York was unbelievably exciting. I know New Yorkers get accused of thinking that our city is the center of the universe, and I know (sort of) that it's not. But at that particular moment in history, there wasn't a more exhilarating place to live. The city was edgy, raw, more dangerous and less civil than it is now, but also coursing with energy. Cocaine and pot were the drugs of choice in the city then, available anywhere anytime. You could have your cocaine delivered, or you could stop by the dry cleaner and pick it up on your way home. It was fun on occasion, but we managed to keep our activity limited and "recreational." The allure faded over time. In part, I think that was our own discipline—we were both particularly sensitive about abusing our bodies—but it was also luck. No one wants to get addicted. We both had friends who lost control, some who battled back to a healthy life and others, sadly, who were swept away.

Going out with John at night was like having a key to the city. He was invited to everything. Doormen bowed and velvet ropes fell when he stepped out of a cab. Sometimes I felt as though I was with Moses, watching the crowd in front of Area or Save the Robots part like the Red Sea. We didn't go out every night, but the opportunity was always there. Monday was the China Club, where the New York Giants partied and Lawrence Taylor was known to do "shots" with fifths of vodka. Tuesday was Nell's, sometimes for dinner, better for dancing. Wednesday heated up with a regular gig at the Roxy. On Thursday you'd try to find Sasha Bardet's moving club, which had its best run on Beach Street. At the Pyramid Club you might find an entire wedding party in drag, while the World had a starry ceiling and great DJs. I liked it more than John did. He went out often, loved the energy, enjoyed being the center of attention, but he had just as good a time hanging out at home with his friends. And both of us valued our sleep, which precluded constant clubbing.

We had people over, but only occasionally. One night we invited some friends over to watch the sixth game of the Red Sox–Mets World Series and the Giants versus the Redskins, which were on at the same time. We stacked two TVs and put out some chips and dip. The guests arrived, we dipped our chips for a bit, and then it was game time. Everyone found a seat, John picked up the remote, and the screen lit up—to reveal the XXX porno tape that *someone* had left in the VCR. John and I went beet red as the fifteen people in our living room watched in stunned silence.

Instinctively, John and I pointed at each other. We'd been doing this for years. Except we both knew that John had left the movie there. He leaped up and pushed the VCR's ON/OFF button practically into the next building. The crowd started breathing again and everyone burst out laughing. John rubbed his hands together and asked, "Does anyone need anything? Beer? More chips?"

Our apartment was indeed the site of some strange sexual adventures—sadly, not all of them ours. One time, a friend came to visit for a few days and brought with him a flight attendant he'd met on his trip. Being good hosts, John and I offered up our rooms. Strangely, he chose John's, though it was the smaller one. We learned why later in the night, after they had retired for the evening and inadvertently (I hope) left the door open a crack. We shouldn't have seen this, but we did: our lusty friend rubbing the sheepskin collar of John's father's official commander in chief leather flight jacket on the bare breasts of his guest. He was whispering seductively something about the "First Coat." Truth. John and I stumbled out the front door and into the stairwell, snorting with laughter. We never said a word about the incident, even when the woman stepped out of the bedroom the next morning wearing only a thong and the aphrodisiac coat.

Another time a friend of John's, a transplanted New Yorker living in San Francisco, was coming to stay with us. He arrived at the apartment one winter afternoon and went out to dinner before I got a chance to meet him. John left me a note saying that he'd given his friend, also named John, the house keys and that I should expect to see him about eleven that night. But he didn't show up. The next morning, as I munched my dry Cap'n Crunch and John inhaled his twenty-nine-grain toast and bowl of Euell Gibbons feed, John explained that his friend was in New York to tell his family he was gay. He was surprised that he hadn't come back the previous night. We showered and started to walk out together, leaving a note for the missing guest. As we stepped out into the hallway, we were greeted by the sight of two gray-trousered legs sticking out of the utility closet. Cuffed and nicely creased. It was a little creepy. Then the legs stirred and our guest stood up and stepped into the light. John, the roommate, introduced us with his usual manners.

"Robert," he said, addressing me formally, "I'd like you to meet my friend John. Who came to New York to come out of the closet." And so he did.

Our problems in those days were small and easily resolved. I learned to leave my pressed shirts at work to avoid drenching them in subway-generated sweat. John struggled with how to hold on to a bicycle. He lived on his bike, using it to get around in all seasons, and had one stolen at least every three months. I've had a number of bikes stolen in the city over the years—it happens, especially to nice shiny new bikes, which was what John always had. But he set some kind of record. He got my bike stolen once, explaining later that he'd left it right outside the window of a diner where he was eating. He couldn't believe it had been pinched. "Did you lock it?" I asked.

"No," he responded, seemingly surprised at the question.

The BGM (bike gone missing) problem annoyed John, but he hated losing his wallet more. It left him all the time. We once drove an hour back to a rest stop on I-95 because he'd tossed it in the garbage pail at McDonald's. He finally solved the problem by buy-ing a wallet that chained to his pants. Making sport of John's seeming absentmindedness was a favorite pastime of all who knew him. I think he wasn't so much absentminded as overbooked. With so much going on all the time, a few things were bound to get lost in the shuffle. And he liked the ribbing he got. It made him accessible and balanced out his intimidating features. In that, it served his purpose: to make people comfortable.

John chose to go to law school because it was the logical thing to do. It's the straightest line to the many different careers, in-cluding social justice and politics, in which he was interested. I think it was also something of a family tradition—that's what the majority of Kennedys did, they went to law school. He encoun-tered a speed bump, though, in the form of the LSATs, the re-quired test for all law-school applicants. He never did that well on standardized tests, but whatever his learning issues, he didn't make excuses. When he got his scores, I asked how he did and he gave me the old thumbs-down. The only time I saw him truly dis-mayed was the day he got rejected from Harvard Law School. He got home and went right to the mail. I'd already noticed that the letter from Harvard was thin—a bad sign. He opened the letter, tossed it on the table, and said darkly, "I'm not going *there*." Then he went to his room and closed the door. He came out the next morning cheerful and calm. And proceeded to get rejected again. It was painful to pull the thin envelopes out of our mailbox—I wanted to hide them. At one point he wondered if he was going to get in anywhere. He worried that the schools he'd applied to as-sumed he wasn't serious about the law. I don't think he wanted to be a lawyer forever, but the law is the logical path to public life in this country and he was committed to doing well. Finally, he got into New York University Law School, a great school and maybe a better place for him than Harvard, where his family name was currency. I was sorry he'd had to go through the wringer but was glad he was staying nearby.

Seven

BACK TO SCHOOL

———

ABOUT THE TIME that our lease on Eighty-sixth Street was expiring, John and I were invited over to his mother's apartment for a casual weekday supper, ostensibly to get a home-cooked meal, Marta-style. As we sat down to eat, I noticed something odd that I'd seen Mrs. Onassis do many times before. As soon as Efigenio ("Effy" Pinhiero was the family's longtime butler and beloved man Friday) served her—he always put her plate down first—Mrs. Onassis lifted her fork and placed it across the plate. This time, since it was just the three of us at the table, I asked, "What's with the fastest-fork-in-the-East thing?"

She explained that it was a custom, one of the myriad protocols of state and home etiquette she'd mastered. Before anyone else at the table could eat, the lady of the table must either take a bite out of something on her plate or simply put her fork on it. I insist on that at home now. Moments later she showed me the real meaning of "hostess." I'm a heavyweight oddball when it comes to food.

Picky doesn't begin to describe my plight. I literally cannot eat most things served at a proper table without gagging. It's an issue that's always made me nervous at dinner parties. My stomach was in a knot that night at the prospect of having to push scallops or veal around my plate under the all-seeing gaze of Mrs. Onassis. And there wasn't a pet in sight to help me. Efigenio came through the kitchen door again, this time smiling like the canary who'd escaped the cat. He placed my plate in front of me and I looked down to see a burned hamburger on a toasted Wonder Bread hamburger roll, with a large mound of white Minute Rice on the side. My favorite meal! Before I could stutter out my gratitude, Mrs. O smiled and waved her hand in the air to stop me. My shoulders dropped an inch, and we all started eating.

As the meal progressed, Mrs. Onassis got to the point: We were there for a reason, it turned out. She suggested that since John was deeply immersed in the work of law school and I had embarked on my own career, perhaps our living together—our extended fraternity run, as it were—wasn't such a good idea. This was done gently but firmly. She even asked whether I'd help John with his schoolwork, if needed, when we lived apart. She ended the dinner with a toast, wishing both John and me a speedy ascent to the top of our respective professions.

This was vintage Mrs. O. She didn't tell John what to do. She presented her opinion in a way that made sense and with the utmost respect for the feelings of everyone involved. It was hard not to see her point: Our lease was ending, John was in law school, and hard work was not what we did best together. John described us, jokingly, as "breaking up," but she was right and we took her advice.

When we moved out, *People* magazine quoted our landlord complaining that the apartment had been abused. An unnamed source told *New York* magazine, "It looked like a herd of yaks had lived there." I'll admit that we'd made several large dings in the plaster walls, the result of some roughhousing gone bad, and that the rug was worn in front of the couch. But we had the walls replastered and the rug cleaned (John's idea—irresponsibility always cost him more than me). So we weren't model tenants. It wasn't the kind of offense that rated national coverage.

I moved to an apartment on West End Avenue with another Brown friend, while John moved alone to a hotel apartment on the East Side. I don't remember the name of it. He worked hard at law school, made a bunch of friends, graduated in 1989, and went to work for the Manhattan District Attorney's Office. He considered an offer to work for the Clinton administration, in the Justice Department, not long after joining the DA. (He'd actually interned for the Reagan administration's Justice Department in Washington, D.C., in the summer of 1987, a move that was seemingly out of Democratic character, but John liked President Reagan and was really just looking to gain some practical experience.) He asked me what I thought about his taking the job. I advised against it, saying it would be a mistake, politically, to hook up with an unproven quantity out of Arkansas. I believed that, but I'm sure I was also rationalizing to keep him in New York. He'd done a stint as a paralegal for an old Kennedy counselor and ex–Democratic National Committee chairman, Charles Manatt, in Los Angeles in the summer of 1988, while he was in law school, and I'd missed him a lot.

As is standard, John began working in the District Attorney's Office before taking the bar exam, that cerebral shakedown cruise all lawyers must survive before practicing. He took the bar exam in late 1989 and flunked. The tabloids had a party, but John shook it off and persevered. He took the exam again and flunked again. This time the experience drove him to drink.

He called me the afternoon he received his second bar exam score. I was living downtown with Frannie by then. A water main had broken on an icy night in January and filled up my duplex basement apartment on West End Avenue like an ice cube tray. I headed downtown for good, Frannie and I forced to live together, despite our misgivings, by an act of God. John's voice was low as he said, "Yo . . . I failed the bar again. Not good."

For the life of me, I couldn't come up with a helpful response. I tried a platitude or two, but John was too frustrated even to mock my words. He finished the conversation by telling me he was going to "haul up north with a bottle of Macallan." He drove his little blue truck, a GMC Typhoon, up to a motel near Lake George, checked in, and slowly drank a bottle of Scotch over the course of the weekend, alone and listening to self-help tapes. I'm not sure the tapes did much good, but he did get a therapist not long after. He found it a great help, allowing him to articulate the enormous complexities of his life without worrying about sounding ungrateful or weak.

When John failed the second time, it seemed to precipitate a crisis of sorts regarding his father. By the age of twenty-nine, his dad had already written a bestseller, won a Purple Heart, and been elected to Congress. One day, about a week after the second no-pass, an older colleague at the District Attorney's Office made some flip comment about John's career relative to his dad's. I don't know exactly what the guy said, and John wasn't about to repeat it, but it hurt. John scowled at me as he told the story, stating adamantly, "I'm not my father."

I shot back, "You're not? Well, who's going to be him, then?"

He smirked appreciatively. I think he was finally ready to come to terms with the subject. His choices were fairly clear: He could drive himself insane trying to compete with the legacy of a legend, or he could figure out a way to live his own life. And from experience, I can tell you that the pressure of a dead father is less than that of a live one. For one thing, you can tell yourself that he would have wanted you to be happy. That's what most loving parents want for their children.

Faced with the district attorney's rule that failing the bar three times got you fired, John hired a tutor and arranged for a special test session, alone and with looser time restrictions. It worked and he passed. He ultimately spent four years as an assistant district attorney. He might have stayed longer—he was good at his job and won all six of the cases he prosecuted—but his celebrity proved a huge hindrance. For one thing, his boss, the respected Robert Morgenthau, was understandably wary about putting John in the courtroom, given the media circus it caused. There were problems with the defendants, too: They would confess to him. They'd confess to win his attention and sympathy. It frustrated John no end. He said they saw him as a potential ally. "They think I can help them," he told me. "So they confide in me—the prosecutor. Greaaaat."

Eventually he decided to abandon the legal profession. To me there's no mystery as to why. He'd never spoken with any passion about being a lawyer. The defendants were giving up their right to remain silent, and thus out of jail, in exchange for a few kind words from him. And every time he set foot in a courtroom, the media put him on trial, too. The guy was not meant to be a lawyer. His departure was not according to plan, though. John wanted to come out of the District Attorney's Office after a successful career corralling big bad guys, much as Rudy Giuliani had done as U.S. attorney. When that proved impossible, he had to shift gears.

He moved to the business world, setting up a corporation, Random Ventures, aptly named to pursue whatever opportunities came down the pike. He considered such things as selling handmade kayaks before coming up with *George*. The idea was his—he could see the rising demand for celebrity journalism, and he knew that politicians filled the bill. Jann Wenner, an old friend of John's, influenced his decision by example.

The premise of *George* was that the juncture of politics and celebrity was an interesting, even important, place. John was born at that juncture. He understood the media better than most and was at ease in the corridors of Washington, D.C. He grew up in the era of Ronald Reagan, living proof that if you can act the part, you can get the role. The civic value of *George* also mattered to John—he wouldn't have published a pure entertainment magazine—and he argued that if you got people interested in politicians, you'd get them interested in politics. Time has proved him right, of course.

John had a good idea—and the courage to put his reputation on the line in a most public way—but he wisely let others come up with the financing for *George*. It's one thing (a very big thing) to risk your name and credibility. It's another to risk the family fortune by pouring millions of dollars into a magazine start-up. So John, who always bought the best but had a pennywise New Englander's grip on his wallet, structured *George* as an earn-out deal. He received his ownership stake based on the success of the project, ending up with a 50 percent share, the maximum possible. Given what his name and presence alone were worth to the magazine, he probably sold himself short.

Eight

HIGH ALTITUDE

———

JOHN CALLED ME at work one slow February afternoon in 1988 and asked if I wanted to go helicopter skiing with him. He'd been offered two slots on a Canadian Mountain Holidays trip in early March. This was prime skiing time in the Canadian Rockies because the sky is clear and the glaciers are stable. The helicopters drop skiers high above the tree line for quadricep-crunching runs through waist-high virgin powder. It took me all of a split second to commit to the trip, despite the fact that I'd have to bust open my piggy bank to go. Skiing was what John and I did best, and the Cariboos, our destination, is one of the sport's holy sites.

Over the next few weeks we gathered the necessary equipment and went to the weight room at the Downtown Athletic Club every other day to get into shape. We took off from JFK on the first Friday evening in March, flying to Detroit and then on to Calgary. I was more excited than I'd ever been for a ski trip, and I get very excited about ski trips.

The headquarters of Canadian Mountain Holidays, called

CMH, is in Banff, Alberta, a long way from anywhere. There were forty-four people scheduled to go on the trip, and we all met Saturday morning in the lobby of a Calgary hotel, where we boarded a bus for a seven-hour drive to the mountains. We arrived at our destination, an unmarked lot in the middle of a forest, early in the afternoon. The bus looked strange out there in the middle of all that nature, a big gaudy chunk of metal in the pristine wilderness. Since neither John nor I was born to sit still, we were downright twitchy coming off the bus, leaping around like escaped pinballs. We began to throw a tennis ball around, trying to loosen up our stiff muscles. An older American man, who turned out to be an accountant from Tulsa, walked over and told us to stop tossing the ball in the air. He said, with a nerdy know-it-all air, that it could damage the helicopter's rotor blades. This was the first of 2,347 bits of advice we would receive from Art Dion over the following week. We smirked a little, but we put away the ball.

Less than thirty seconds later, a helicopter came *whup-whup-whupping* out of the mountains like a mutant locust. It was to carry us, in groups of eleven, to the Cariboo Lodge, which is accessible in winter only by copter. Being polite and instinctively eager to ingratiate ourselves with the old-timers, John and I let everyone else go up first. Bad idea: All the massage time slots were filled by the time we got there. Finally it was our turn and we climbed aboard with our load of gear. The Bell 212 twin-engine helicopter swooped up into the canyons and alighted on a helipad adjoining a multibuilding complex that was the Cariboo Lodge. We were at 3,600 feet above sea level, in a small clearing cut out of a landslide-protected swath of forest. The lodge, though not fancy, was a monument to physical comfort. A gym, a game room, a screening room, and more had been hauled up the mountains by truck in the

Hip-hopping in the Canadian Rockies. (Courtesy of Mark Chitty)

summer months, mostly to languish unused during ski season because the skiing wipes you out like a hundred-foot wave.

Our fellow skiers were a colorful cast of international characters, almost all repeat visitors to the Cariboos. John and I were especially intrigued by a James Bond type named Michael Jack. An ex-mercenary herb farmer who'd left his carbine in Yemen and settled in Zimbabwe with his wife and four daughters, Michael told spellbinding tales of his days at Sandhurst, England's military academy, and his nights on patrol in Yemen, working for the government's Special Forces. If he was to be believed—and we did believe him—he'd been a killing machine of sorts before turning to

Our mercenary/ herb farming friend Michael Jack, with us up at the Cariboo Lodge in Canada. (Courtesy of Mark Chitty)

herb farming. A fine skier, he was as cool as the breeze, witty, and a bit scary.

The most playful members of the crew were a group of Iranian royalists out of Houston whom we dubbed the Persian World Party Tour (PWPT). Not surprisingly, we'd gone to school with a relative of a PWPT member, the lovely Ayshe Farman-Farmain, and they adopted us right off into their playgroup. The PWPT enjoyed life unabashedly, consuming a case of vintage Montrachet each night with dinner and a box of Cuban cigars with dessert. After-dinner activities included cerebral warfare over the backgammon table, with the PWPT hurling Farsi epithets at one another while conversing with the rest of us in perfect English. The power of history was confirmed when the French and Swiss skiers immediately squared off against the British guests. John and I ended up

John smiles when I choke on a Cuban "heater" in the Cariboo Lodge. (Courtesy of Mark Chitty)

with the cricket-bat wielders, since they shared our sense of humor and had the Special Forces guy. There were several Germans, too, seemingly skiing on a different mountain, one that was dark and serious.

Although everyone wined and dined and ached together in the evenings, during the day there were some geopolitical skirmishes. On the first day of skiing, the top French skier, an instructor from the world-famous Val d'Isère resort, somehow fell behind. In a mad dash to rejoin his group, he ran his skis under a hidden branch, his bindings released, and he flew through the air like a tricolor human rocket. Just like a cartoon, he whistled thirty feet down the hill and disappeared into a snowbank. When he emerged, the Frenchman was redder than the rooster on his hat. He haughtily refused a British offer of help to find his skis. There were two minutes of dead, pained silence while he collected his belongings and huffed and puffed away. Then the Brits, and John and I with them, fell over in tears. Waterloo relived.

Each day of the trip was the same: In the morning, in groups of eleven, we'd be taken by helicopter to an altitude of 10,000 feet or so and dropped, sometimes literally, on a glacier. The guides had some 575 square miles of skiing terrain to choose from, and we skied a different route every run. The four guides skied in front, on the lookout for avalanches and crevasses. We were warned not to ski off on our own, and in the trees everyone had to ski in pairs. We also wore transponders to help rescuers locate us under the snow, in the event that became necessary.

The risks of jumping out of a helicopter and skiing down the face of a glacier are fairly obvious. Nothing is perfectly safe, and we trusted in our ability and in CMH's expertise. The rewards of the adventure are harder to describe and of a different magnitude altogether. The physicist Fritjof Capra, in his book *The Tao of Physics,* suggests that alpine skiing is the closest we mortals can get to the higher peace attained by Zen masters through a lifetime of meditation. And this was the purest form of skiing, on mountains untouched by man. For us it was bliss, some kind of rare transcendence rooted in nature and our own physicality.

Which isn't to say there weren't a few temporal issues. On my first run, I tumbled down the mountain like a sneaker in a dryer. I was a human Popsicle by noon. There was snow up me bum and no possibility of warming up until the end of the day. But discomfort is relative, and I was jolted out of my chill when our young German guide took off between two trees into the thickest, steepest forest I'd ever seen. These were not glades, mind you, but tightly packed trees, each circled by a deadly tree well, set on a steep incline. Tree wells are deep, wind-carved sinkholes of snow that spread out from the base of a tree. They're a skier's nightmare: If you fall into one and there's no one to help you out, you can die. Then there's the tree itself to consider. A minute or so after our guide disappeared, we heard him yodel happily far below. We looked at each other in disbelief, a group of expert and cocky skiers paralyzed by fear. John, who was wearing the team's safety back-pack at the time, waved everybody on. I took off just ahead of him, and we skied together down into the forest. The snow under the pine boughs was lighter and softer than I can describe. About a hundred yards into the woods we were letting out whoops of joy (though quietly, so as not to cause any avalanches).

Suddenly a snow snake (an old ski legend not unlike the Loch Ness monster) got ahold of one of John's skis. He lost the ski and continued on, barreling another thirty-five feet on one ski and barely avoiding several pine trees en route. A harrowing few sec-onds later, he came to a stop in a whirlwind of fluff, laughing at his misadventure. He popped off his remaining ski in order to hunt for the missing one. We bellowed down the hill that we were de-layed, but heard nothing back except our own echo. Still worried about avalanches, we stopped yelling and started rooting around in the four-foot-deep powder. The ski was nowhere to be found. The hunt was exhausting, our fatigue compounded by the altitude. Desperation arrived after five minutes, and tears flowed after ten. That was the only time I ever saw John cry. He wasn't afraid, he was furious with himself and frustrated that he was holding up forty-three other people, at ten thousand feet, frozen, with no en-ergy and only one ski. Seconds before both our nervous systems blew out, I found the ski about ten feet below us, a yard beneath the surface. John trudged down to get it, snatching it out of my

"Which way is down?" John enjoys the view of the Rocky Mountains in Canada. (Courtesy of the author)

grasp as though I'd been hiding it. He was embarrassed, unnecessarily, so I slapped a hangdog look on my face and said, "My fault. Won't happen again." He smiled and refastened his ski.

We took our time catching up, having learned the dangers of rushing from the French rocket, and reached the chopper about twenty minutes late. Our guide, Bernhard Ehmann, ripped into John, implying that his mishap had endangered the team. This was totally unfair. Everyone took a spill now and then. And I was clearly the laissez-faire fellow in our group, while John and Bernard shared a quasi-military approach to safety and preparedness. John had been the most attentive listener at the avalanche training session, and he and I had volunteered to carry the safety pack for the group. We were also in charge of opening and closing the helicopter door on each sortie, a task we'd earned by virtue of our relative youth and size. It was like stepping into a two-hundred-mile-an-hour blizzard and wrestling an ice-cold manhole cover, twenty-eight times a day. In our group, John was clearly the biggest Boy Scout with the most badges, but he earned Bernhard's wrath that day. Even more unfair, though I enjoyed it, was Bernhard's decision to make me his model skier and best friend. After John and I got our skis fastened to the rack on the side of the helicopter, Bernhard stared down at John from his jump seat and yelled to the assembled crew, "If vee can elee-minate zee human factor and cover effry conteengensy, vee then have luck on owah side." John being the human factor.

That night, as we lay like big sourdough pretzels in bed, too sore to move, John mused for half an hour about how in the world Bernhard could like me and not him. I didn't say anything, but it was clear that Bernhard liked John. Like so many others, he was just making John jump through some "Are you a real person?" hoops to prove his worth.

Mornings began at seven A.M., when a cowbell rang to announce the start of stretching class. Reasoning that we weren't cows, we always slept in, grabbing another three minutes of rest. The next ten minutes were spent slowly, slowly creaking out of bed. Though John and I were among the youngest in the group and were in good shape, we were skiing to the point of near paralysis each day thanks to several clever marketing ploys on the part of CMH. The first was its frequent-flyer program, which was a near obsession with many on the trip: For every million vertical

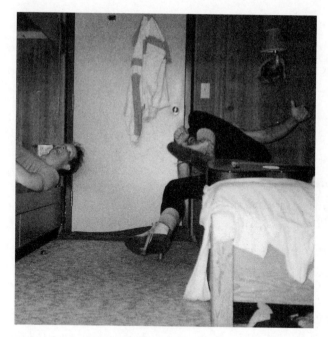

In praise of Advil: John and I pretend to suffer muscle cramps for the camera after a hard day skiing on the glacier. In fact, we could barely move. (Courtesy of the author)

feet skied, CMH would give you a sweet, one-piece ski suit with the CMH logo on it. Art Dion had four of them. There was a weekly incentive, too—to ski 200,000 vertical feet. For this milestone, rarely achieved, you received a gold pin and got your name on the wall. The conditions that week were stellar, and the hardcore heli-skiers were scrapping for every extra foot.

Art Dion, the guy John and I originally nominated for head lame-o, became our savior. Each night before bed, he'd give us a little bag of vitamins and herbal anti-inflammatories. In the morning we'd query him like a prophet on ways to reduce muscle soreness. Art paid for a double room each time he visited, sleeping in one bed and laying out his remedies on the other. Bless him. As for the benefits of stretching, we found that the best "stretch" for tight muscles was the terror-induced adrenaline rush that accompanied

Lunchtime without a fireplace? Canadian hospitality apparently stops at the tree line when heli-skiing! (Courtesy of Mark Chitty)

the first jump out of the chopper in the morning. By the time you landed on the glacier, everything was working.

We ate lunch at the top of whatever mountain we happened to be on at noon, above the friggin' tree line, with no lodge, no fire-place, and definitely no hot cocoa. Rest room? A dream. John loved those lunches, reveling in the sparse ruggedness of it all. I, on the other hand, tried to conjure up Jacuzzis and burgers with my imagination. We skied an average of ten long, glorious runs a day, the conditions so unusually good that the 200,000-foot holy grail was within reach. In fact, twenty-two of the forty-four skiers made it, a CMH record. I missed the figure by thirty lousy feet, but they kindly rounded up, giving me a pin and a place adjacent to John on a plaque in the lodge. I'll probably never see it again, Florida being so nice and toasty in the winter, but I love knowing it's there.

———

My family has a house in Utah, the home of Wasatch powder, indisputably the best snow in the world and a great hook for getting friends to visit. Over the years, John and I had many an adventure on the slopes of Snowbird, Alta, Park City, and Deer Valley. As I mentioned, John was Olympic timber on the mountains. I know because we skied with an ex–Olympic team member at Deer Valley once. She, the stunning blond official Deer Valley ambassador of skiing, Heidi Voelker, was a friend of Kevin Ruff's, a mate on that particular trip, and she told me on the chairlift that John could have been a pro skier. You can imagine how painful it was for me to hear that. I have to admit I never shared the compliment with him. I did prompt Heidi to say who she thought was the best skier in our group, and she took me down another notch by saying that the best skier was my sister. All in the family, at least.

My folks' house is in the valley that makes up Salt Lake City, so each morning of every trip we'd pack up the car and head south to Little Cottonwood Canyon, to ski at Snowbird and Alta, or north to Park City and Deer Valley. On the first day of one all-guy trip, five of us stuffed ourselves into a rental car and headed up the serpentine access road to Snowbird and Alta. My foot was pressed hard to the accelerator when, about halfway up the canyon, we heard a loud pop. The car came to a halt. We piled out, flanked by a sheer rock wall on one side and a deep ravine on the other. Being the pack of Ivy League softies that we were, none of us knew any more about cars than how to open the hood. So we did that and noticed that the wire from the accelerator pedal had frayed and broken at the point where it was attached to the lever on the carburetor that allows gas to enter the engine. We waited for help. And waited some more. Finally, John chipped in with a one-word solution: "Sweetarts."

I happened to be standing in front of the car, its large hood open and puny engine exposed, popping Sweetarts in my mouth. They're one of my favorite food groups, and I travel with them all the time. We looked at John, hoping his next words would be more informative than the first one. He just repeated, "Sweetarts."

The light dawned. It was pure MacGyver. I took a Sweetart and placed it under the lever, slightly opening the valve that supplied fuel to the engine. Paul Oberbeck suggested two might be better, as the hill was steep in places. Two it was. The car started with a roar. I threw it into gear and kept my foot hard on the brake. Four harrowing minutes later, we careened into the Snowbird valet parking zone, right up to the resort's front door. A surprised-looking crew of attendants came rushing over, waving their arms and barking out the "You can't park here" policy their jobs depended on. My passengers, except for John, leaped out of the car as if it were leaking fuel and made for the lodge. I wasn't sure how to handle the parking issue, but John, using his best snowboardspeak, had already assembled the valets in front of the car to explain our situation. He motioned for me to pop the hood and then waved his arm over the carburetor, saying, "Duuudes, check this out."

When they saw the candy, the valets rendered their collective opinion: "Sweet."

The head man added, "You can leave it right here. Cool."

We nodded our thanks, barely, in keeping with the no-shape, no-color, no-emotion minimalism of snowboarding, and walked inside, never to see the car again. The rental car company arranged for a replacement to be there by 4:15. Which was also cool.

———

The following year Frannie and I invited a bunch of Italian friends to Utah. John joined us midway through the ten-day trip. With him was his girlfriend at the time, Julie Baker, a sweet-natured, strikingly beautiful model. The next day, a March sparkler, we began our morning on the moguls at Alta, taking advantage of the nightly snow dump. The bumps had already been carved, and the fresh snow made them like big fluffy meringues covered in buttery vanilla frosting. I could slam my large frame down again and again without fear. I had the B-52's' "Bushfire" cranking on my Walkman and the sun at my back, so I could admire my shadow on the way down. I had my wife and friends, and Julie Baker, too—who's easier on the eyes than a pile of hundred-dollar bills. I asked her to ski over and watch me, suggesting that I'd ski better knowing that Beauty itself was backing me up. And I was right. I ripped it—two hundred yards of sinew-busting, tight-turned mogul dusting. Sun, song, snow, and personal glory. I didn't even turn around, skiing down to the lift on a cushion of bliss.

Unbeknownst to me, I had awoken the ugly troll in John. Our group caught up and I could see right away that John was bristling a bit, avoiding eye contact with me. He'd taken my prowess in the bumps as a personal affront. Our next run was down steeper, untracked terrain, and the group merrily attacked the slope. Eventually John and I found ourselves alone on a ledge overlooking a particularly nasty bit of hill, with flat light. He gave me a grumpy nod and took off at high speed, determined to show me how the

On the deck at the Snowbird Lodge. (Courtesy of Dave Eikenberry)

mountain should be skied. Several nice turns later, John entered an unseen gully, one that had been obscured by the terrain above it. He sped into it and then out. Unfortunately, he left his skis under a branch on the way out, much like the Frenchman had done years before. He flew through the air with the greatest of ease, landing in a clump. I skied down slowly to check him out. He got up, swaying like a newborn deer, his sunglasses missing a lens and sitting askew on his face. Physically, he seemed fine, though he'd hit his head hard on the snowpack. I asked if he was okay. He said something like "Wha . . . ? Huh? Oh yeah, hold on."

For five long, mountain-cold minutes he composed himself and readjusted his equipment. He'd look up every thirty seconds or so, acknowledge my polite smile, and grumble, "Dick."

As if I'd done something wrong. I suggested that he take a

break and offered to go in with him so that it would remain our little secret. My compassion infuriated him, as I'd known it would. Waving me off, he skied away in the direction of the base lodge to get new sunglasses, unwilling to admit defeat as long as the day was still young. (Any guy who has skied with another guy knows exactly what I'm talking about. It's a mad competition. Who's stronger, faster, and better? I can't walk normally for weeks after a three-day ski outing with the boys—we pretty much try to kill one another.) John and I almost called a truce on our last trip to Deer Valley. We spoke like two old Cold War negotiators, at the top of the lift on our first run. I suggested that we were equal skiers and we could relax for a run or two. He agreed, but it wasn't much fun. Before we got back to the top for the second run, we were lobbying our chairlift mates to pick the better skier.

For us, competition was a fundamental element of friendship. But it wasn't a ferocious contest of egos, as it seemed on the football field in Hyannis Port. It was one of the ways, maybe the purest way, we connected to each other. Some friends have heart-to-hearts over dinner. We didn't do that. We played racquetball. And skied. And talked a little between bantering. People will ask me questions about John sometimes and not understand how I don't know the answer. Well, I never asked the question. Ours was a bond forged in activity (though it was more than that, too), and we enjoyed each other's company most when we were wholly engaged in something physical.

As John skied off with his sunglasses still askew, he yelled back that he'd meet us at Chick's Place, the mid-mountain eatery at Alta. Not long after, while our group made its way to lunch, we heard John yelling from the chairlift, "Hey! Wait up. Wait uuuuuupp!"

Which didn't sound like him at all, indicating to me that he was still dazed from his fall. We found a flat spot under the chair-lift and settled on the trail to wait. With a fresh set of sunglasses on his head and an introspective chairlift ride under his belt, John took off down the steep hill like a shot, taking the fall line directly toward us. Bad luck intact, he hit a gnarled twig poking out of the snow and wiped out completely. Skiers call it a "yard sale," because all your equipment flies off and lands scattered about the hill, spread out as if for sale. John then slid a good thirty yards at increasing speed until he wrapped around the lone sapling on the slope, a little like a wet newspaper. He yelled, with all the anger and frustration left in his body, "Littellllll!"

Everyone looked at me, perhaps not seeing the connection. Victory in hand, I suggested that the others go on to lunch, and I'd wait for John. He schussed down soon enough, and to my dismay his sunglasses were cockeyed again. Nobody likes to see his buddy lose his dignity. I adjusted his glasses while he snorted appreciatively and then we skied to lunch.

I took my turns as the goat, too. Once, after a monster day on the slopes of Park City, we settled in for some après-ski food and cocktails at a Mexican restaurant on the plaza. Already naturally doped up from the day's exhilarating activities, I had three margaritas and got silly drunk. I handed the car keys over to my sister, while John and another friend, Dave Eikenberry, made fun of my sodden state. I giggled like a little kid in the backseat and suffered a harsh hangover the next morning. We headed out again for another big day of skiing and an encore visit to Marita's Cantina. We sat at the same table and had the same friendly waitress. I ordered a margarita, swearing that I was going to have only one. She looked at me strangely and suggested I try getting some tequila for my drink. You see, in Utah back then, they didn't put the liquor in the drinks. The waitress brought you a "setup," and you had to go to the control point to buy the minibottle to make a real cocktail out of it. Meaning I'd been hammered the night before on the pure power of suggestion. Needless to say, it was a long evening.

———

I had a running dialogue with Mrs. Onassis over the years as to the best name for John's and my generation. We were not quite baby boomers and not quite Gen Xers. We were the first generation in many to grow up without a draft, much less a war to fight. Too young for Vietnam and too old for the Gulf War, we were just pups during the civil rights movement, the sixties, Watergate, and other societal upheavals. We'd come of age in a time of calm and plenty and been coddled to near apathy. Mrs. O and I agreed upon the title "the Inheritors." Which was, in fact, a reasonable name for our generation as a whole, and particularly for John. When I told him what we'd come up with, he snorted and said, "I'll say!"

One of the many things John had inherited was use of the family estate down in Palm Beach. The house was designed by Addison Mizner, the legendary architect who created Palm Beach in the 1920s. It had been in the family since 1933, purchased by John's grandfather Joe for $100,000. It was a beautiful place, with ocean views, a pool, a tennis court, and a croquet lawn. Rodman Wanamaker, who built the house, called it La Guerida, but in the early 1960s it was known as the Winter White House. It wasn't used much by the time we went, but the extended family had a sort of time-share arrangement that allotted John and Caroline the first two weeks in March. John, his new girlfriend, Christina Haag (a Brown alumna he'd had a crush on—or in John's words, a "sneaker for"—for a long time), Frannie, and I flew down, rented a convertible, and immediately got lost in West Palm Beach. We were puzzling over a map at a stoplight when a man in the car behind us, too polite to honk, stuck his head out the window and yelled, "Don't get no greener." I love that line.

The house was grand but eerie. As I remember it, there was a vast living room running almost the length of the house with a large fireplace and a stairway up to the master bedrooms in the middle. The wall facing the beach had multiple glass doors and windows that opened onto a simple lawn with thick green grass. Not a lot of fancy gardening. We made camp in the southwestern corner of the manse, near the tennis court and pool. That first night, Frannie wanted a snack and sent me off to search for the kitchen. I've never been afraid of the dark, but I was spooked. I passed a small study and stepped inside to look for a good book. The room was filled with memorabilia and Kennedy lore—framed speeches, photo albums, knickknacks from high office. It was like a mini–congressional library, dark and musty and stuck in time. There was nothing remotely similar to this at 1040 or on the Vineyard or in Mrs. Onassis's little farmhouse in Peapack, New Jersey, which I visited just once. I think Mrs. O, knowing that the past can be oppressive, had limited its presence in her own homes. I clearly remember a framed speech by Teddy Kennedy leaning on a bookcase. It was a plea of sorts, a passionate defense of liberalism that had clearly been written during the height of Reagan's conservative administration. I was already sensing spirits, and the speech made me sad. It was a bugler's call to battles never finished, a reminder of soldiers fallen. There were big pictures of John's father and Bobby Kennedy on the walls. The whole house, as I resumed my search for the kitchen, felt like a monument to lost possibilities.

John and I talked about the weird energy of the house the next day. He was shaken, too, unable to dust off the cobwebs, real and emotional, that seemed everywhere. We spent as much time as possible outdoors.

The house was sold in 1995, furniture and all, not because it was haunted but because it had become financially impractical. I think of it often now—I've even dreamed about it—and would love to walk there again, late at night. I don't really believe in ghosts, but then again, I can't imagine a more likely place to encounter John's spirit.

———

Extreme sports and *adventure travel* were catchphrases of the early nineties, but the only really extreme thing that John and I ever did was go skydiving. (I guess you could count helicopter skiing because it was *extremely* fun.) I probably wouldn't have come up with the idea on my own, and I can't say I enjoyed it, but as soon as it was over I loved telling the story.

It started, as so many adventures with John did, with an out-of-the-blue phone call late one night. John's great friend George Shurrell, whom he'd met at NYU Law School and who ended up working with Maurice Tempelsman in Africa, was in town and wanted to realize an old dream of parachuting. I remember the call clearly because it ruined my chance for a good night's sleep. John began: "Yo, Rob."

"Yes, Goatboy?" I responded warily, hearing something up in his voice.

"Me, George, and Eddie Hill are going skydiving tomorrow and we need some ballast," he said.

"What time?" I asked, cringing.

"Six-thirty A.M."

"Jesus. That's cold. Where do I go?"

"We'll swing by in Eddie's van." He added, "No showering and eating after we buzz."

I started to protest, but he just said, "Are ya coming?"

He may as well have said straight out, "Do you have any *co-jones?*" To me this was a ball check. I said yes.

They arrived right on time the next morning in a beat-up old van driven by Ed, a good buddy of John's from Andover. Ed, now a prominent lawyer out West, was just coming out of a hippie phase and the van was a remnant of trips gone by. We headed deep into western New Jersey, to Pittstown, where we found Skydive East inhabiting a homegrown airstrip with the improbably grand name of Alexandria Field. We took a three-hour preparation course, me cheering inwardly at the rain outside that was sure to keep us grounded. After the classroom session, during which we were required to sign our lives away on quadruplicated insurance forms, we suited up and headed outside.

Next was jump-and-roll practice: You stand on top of two stacked blue plastic milk crates and leap off, attempting to roll along the ground into a standing position. I'm still not entirely clear on the motion. I stopped paying attention when the instructor pointed out that the actual landing was more like jumping off a two-story building but that you can't practice that. Without paramedics standing by, I guess he meant. As we leaped from the milk crates, a jalopy of an aircraft was rolled out of the hangar and cranked up. We were going up in the original *Spirit of St. Louis.*

By then, the rain had stopped, the morning clouds had blown east, and the sky was entirely blue. My emotions, which I sometimes store in my stomach, were roiling: I didn't want to hurl myself out of an airplane. I wasn't about to back out. It didn't look as though the rain would return. The only thing I could hope for now was to live. I could see that Ed was thinking along the same lines, though John and George remained gung-ho.

The noise from the ancient plane was deafening. We said a few words to the gap-toothed pilot as we climbed in, but he just revved the engines by way of response. So many people had climbed into this craft before us that the corrugated steel floor had lost its corrugation. The four of us huddled in the cabin with our bearded jumpmaster as the pilot began the slow, circling ascent to one mile. There (which is to say, nowhere) the jumpmaster asked who wanted to go first. John answered, "I got it."

And within thirty seconds he'd hurled himself out of the plane and into the great blue sky. George raised his hand next, his testosterone on his sleeve, and made the valiant leap as well. At that point, the jumpmaster queried Ed, who had turned the mottled green color of his van. Ed, choking down the bile, muttered, "Of course, dude. The faster I get down, the better."

Then it was my turn. The jumpmaster signaled me to go, though it wasn't the "go" you're envisioning. We were not leaping out a big door in the side of the plane the way they do in the movies. No, we had to crawl out the small passenger door and onto an eighteen-square-inch piece of rusty steel that was welded to the plane's wheel cover. Then hold on to the wing strut with no goggles. Picture, if you will, a scared 230-pound man clinging to a plane's wing strut a mile above the ground. I mention 230 pounds because I was five pounds above the recommended limit for our T-10 parachutes, military surplus from World War II. I was assured it was no problem—far bigger fellas than I had jumped successfully.

I followed my instructions as if my life depended on it (duh), releasing my grip, arching my back, and counting to five. I tumbled backward as though I'd been flicked off the wing, my eyes shut like bank-vault doors until I sensed a tug at my shoulders. That meant my main chute had opened successfully. I unclenched my eyes and started laughing. Jonathan Livingston Whiteboy! The feeling was amazing—extreme freedom. And relief. Because if the main parachute hadn't opened, we'd been told to engage in a nine-point maneuver meant to get the little reserve chute out and away from the tangled main chute. I would probably have gone fetal midway through step two. Even assuming I'd managed to get to the reserve chute, it was made for a good-size dog, not an oversize human. The instructors had breezily warned us that if the reserve chute deployed, our legs would break at touchdown.

Below me, I watched first John and then George land. The radio attached to my reserve chute began to yap at me. "Feet together! Feet together! Feet together!"

The urgent voice on the radio was no doubt aware that I was over the suggested weight limit for the chute, a fact that had been conveniently overlooked when my credit card cleared. As I neared the ground, the voice grew more insistent. I could just hear John's and George's laughter coming into range when I hit the ground. And not like a ton of bricks. I hit like a 230-pound sack of human, landing in a cornfield with both legs and feet together. My left foot found a furrow, but my right foot didn't. Like overstretched guitar strings, several muscle strands attached to my right knee went *boiing*. The pain was sharp and immediate but was gone a moment later, at least until the next day. The Skydive East welcoming committee, a beautiful Australian girl, ran up and planted a congratulatory kiss right on my lips. This had the effect of momentarily obscuring any pain. Sweet Eddie the Eaglet came down seconds later. And he did look like a sack of potatoes, bouncing a good foot and a half off the ground upon impact.

We shared a round of high fives and hugs. We did it! Back at the airport, we were presented with a bumper sticker, a certificate, and a report card of sorts—a little flight log that determined whether we were ready for the next level, free-falling. The initial novice jump we'd done started with a five-second free fall, after which a tether on the plane yanked the chute open. The next step took you up twice as high and let you fall freely for up to a minute, leaving the rip-cord pulling up to you. John's report card was glowing and he became teacher's pet that day, earning the right to free-fall on his next jump. (It never happened.) George got the go-ahead as well. Ed and me? We got stuffed. The instructor wrote in my logbook that I looked like a "beagle tossed from a pickup truck." I was crestfallen, although of course I just stuck my chin up. Before getting back in the van, we formed a line at the phone booth to call our beloveds back in New York and inform them of our "alive" status. It was easy to promise I'd never do that again.

Nine

RITES OF PASSAGE

———

SOMETIME IN THE mid-1980s, people started getting married. I knew that people got married, of course, but I didn't take any notice until I'd participated in a few weddings myself. The marriage of John's sister, Caroline, to Ed Schlossberg was one of the first I attended. And it set the bar high. Not only was it elegant and emotional, it was unpretentiously, unexpectedly fun.

John and Caroline were as emotionally close as they were temperamentally different. Respectful and protective of each other, they had the kind of bond that parents wish for their children. I never spent a lot of time with Caroline—she rolled her eyes a lot when John and I were together, which seemed right, given that she was his elder sister and far more serious—but she graciously invited Frannie and me and a bunch of John's other friends to her big day.

The wedding was held on July 19, 1986, on a warm, sunny afternoon in Hyannis Port. Frannie and I stayed at a bed-and-breakfast in town the night before, arriving near midnight after an eight-hour, traffic-filled drive from New York. This drive was made all the more annoying by Frannie, who spent hours worrying aloud about her forty-dollar dress from Casual Corner. I considered leaving her at the McDonald's in Milford, Connecticut.

Interestingly, although Caroline was always the more reticent of the two, she planned a much bigger, more inclusive wedding than John did ten years later. No doubt that had something to do with the fact that Mrs. Onassis was still alive and knew how much joy a big festive ritual can bring to an extended family. The "family" in this case included not just Kennedys and Schlossbergs but their friends and also many members of John F. Kennedy's administration, men and women who had known Caroline since she was a baby. The ceremony took place at a church in Centerville, Massachusetts. At the last minute Frannie decided that maybe a hat would help, and we were almost late while she dashed into a shop in town and bought a purple straw thing with flowers. After church we went back to the family compound in Hyannis Port, where two big tents had been set up. What can I say? It was a happy, gorgeous event, everyone excited for Caroline and Ed and glad to be celebrating in the name of love.

I got to meet the globe's biggest testosterone warehouse, Arnold Schwarzenegger. I was pleased to note that I was maybe an inch taller. We shook hands and he scowled at me, which I took as a compliment. John liked Arnold a lot and found our "big man" posturing funny, especially considering how big Arnold actually was.

Soon enough the dinner gong rang and the whole party moved toward the enormous white tent where dinner was being served, buffet-style. After finding our table, I went with John to get some food and found myself standing next to Mrs. Onassis's sister, Lee Radziwill. John, the respectful nephew, introduced us, a bit gingerly I thought. She gave me a steely once-over and then basically dismissed me with a sneer. John looked as surprised as I was. But since I hadn't had time to offend her yet, I just assumed she'd probably met one too people that day and needed some food. Mrs. Radziwill complimented John on his handsome best man's outfit, a cheerful deep violet Perry Ellis jacket and white pants number put together by William Ivey Long. Then she turned her attention back to the service line. And a weird thing happened. As she passed a silver tray that was part of the dazzling spread laid out by the New York caterer Glorious Food, the Sterno can underneath went out with an audible sputter. John and I both saw this happen. I looked around to see if any other flames were flickering in the breeze. No breeze. I checked to see if the fuel had run out. Plenty of pinkish jelly left in the tin. John looked at me. That didn't happen, did it? We took some chicken from the tray and went to sit down. A little shiver flashed down my spine.

A roving videographer provided a warmer touch, walking about with a video camera and capturing the guests' good wishes on film. He arrived at our table late in the dinner, just as Caroline was visiting. Asked to say something for the camera, I said, "May you live and love and pass on as Will and Ariel Durant."

John looked at me as though I were crazy. He said, "What are you talking about?"

So I had to tell him the moving story of Will and Ariel Durant, the renowned husband-and-wife team of philosopher-historians who wrote *The Story of Civilization*. Two brilliant individuals, they worked together for decades, winning a Pulitzer Prize and the Pres-

Lee Radziwill, Jacqueline Kennedy Onassis's sister, stepping out in New York City in 1997. My introduction to her didn't go well. (Courtesy of Mitchell Gerber/Corbis)

idential Medal of Freedom. They had a long and famously loving marriage. In 1981, at the age of ninety-six, Will was admitted to the hospital for surgery. Worried for Will's survival, Ariel stopped eating and died shortly thereafter. When Will heard that his beloved Ariel had passed on, his heart stopped beating. As I finished telling this tale, with a catch in my voice, John continued to look at me as though I'd been caught with the caterer's silverware in my pocket. Caroline looked at me sweetly, gave John a sisterly glare, and said, "That's nice, Rob. Thank you."

John gave a now-famous toast at that wedding, welcoming Ed into the family. "All my life there has just been the three of us,

Mummy, Caroline, and I," he began. And finished with a heartfelt welcome to the fourth member of his family. I remember being surprised at the depth of John's emotions, because I hadn't spent much time around him and his sister. Some years later, just before his own marriage, he wrote in *George* that "the crises and isolation of a public life create a sense of shared burden that can bring a couple closer." I think that also explains why Mrs. Onassis, Caroline, and John were so close.

At the end of the evening there was a fireworks display, a gift to the couple from George Plimpton. By then, though, the sparkling day had been overrun by a classic Cape Cod fog. The crowd gathered at the edge of the lawn, near the beach, to watch the eagerly awaited program. George was handed a microphone. We heard the thud of the first firework's rocket launch off the beach. The fog flashed a luminous pink. George quietly announced the name of the shell. After the fifth or so firework exploded unseen, Plimpton glumly began to describe each shell, telling us what it *would* look like if we could see it. The wedding guests would hear a *whoosh*, then George would say, with his patrician accent, "That was an imperial dragonflower, a bouquet of comet sparklers complemented by a central burst of red and gold and a stunning concussion. Just spectacular." The sky would turn reddish, the smoke would swirl, and then everything went back to gray.

To encourage him, we all exclaimed oohs and aahs on cue, looking up excitedly as if the fireworks were right in front of our eyes. Picture several hundred people huddled up against the dunes, marveling loudly at nothing. It was great fun. As the crowd's cheers grew, George's spirits rose. By the rousing finale, a particularly large and loud blur of pastel-colored smoke, his

Mutual friend John Hare's wedding—I won best man for this one. (Courtesy of Clare Hare)

voice and mood reached a crescendo. And we, the viewers, knew we'd participated in something much better than a fireworks display.

Joseph Campbell, one of Mrs. Onassis's favorite authors, said that humanity is given definition by its rituals. Weddings were such a big part of our life from 1985 to 1995 that we were like one big traveling wedding party. John was the best man for at least five grooms over the years, including his duties as "best dude" for Chris Oberbeck when he married Liz Birkelund. He was not my best man when the time came, because Frannie and I decided to ask our siblings to stand with us. But as my wingman, he hosted a memorable bachelor party and gave a teary toast at our rehearsal dinner.

Encore! Encore! John Hare's bachelor party high jinks at the Iguana Grill in 1987. (Courtesy of the author)

The early weddings were the hardest, involving brain-cell-busting bachelor parties and days-long nuptial celebrations. By the time we were thirty, the words *bachelor party* scared the snot out of all of us. John Hare's dusk-to-dawn New York club crawl entered the annals of pain, followed by a memorable fete for Chris Oberbeck, whom we referred to as the king of Connecticut for his regal countenance. John arranged for Chris's party to begin on a Friday afternoon on Forty-second Street and Eighth Avenue in New York in a rented Winnebago. Our crew of about fifteen guys headed up to John's mother's estate on Martha's Vineyard, called Red Gate Farm, for the weekend, but we missed the last ferry out of Woods Hole, as usual. So we detoured back to Hyannis Port to spend the night. The senator was there when we arrived. He sat with us up on the widow's walk of one of the houses until the wee hours, telling hilarious tales with the voice and delivery of a member of Parliament. We took a ferry to the Vineyard the next morning and partied until dawn on Sunday. Ouch. John escaped to his bedroom before the sun came up, but he mused the next day, as he sometimes did after these raucous events, that someone in the group would prove to be his Judas. He knew it was possible that someone might turn and concoct a false tale to sell to the press. It never happened, though, because his friends were loyal.

Frannie and I decided to get married in 1991, no surprise to anyone around us. Still, we were excited and our friends were more than willing to raise the flag of celebration in our honor. We planned an April wedding, at an Old World, now-defunct club in Battery Park. I asked seven good friends, including John, to be my ushers. At a rowdy Christmas party given by John's friends Kevin and Helen Ward a few months before the event, John grabbed Frannie by the shoulders and asked, "Do you realize you're marrying Rob Littell?" Like I was Alexander the Great or something. Now, *that* is a wingman.

He came through on the bachelor party, too, inviting everyone up to the Vineyard for a party that was a reprise of Chris's. All went according to plan: We rented the Winnebago, drove to the ferry, and missed the ferry. John was already on the Vineyard, waiting for his mates to arrive, and when we didn't show by midnight, he called Frannie in New York.

"Hey, Frannie, it's John," he started off. "Sorry to call so late. Um, do you know where those guys are?"

We were sitting in a bar overlooking the dock in Woods Hole, having abandoned the Winnebago for a motel. We caught the first ferry out the next morning, played nine holes of golf in West

My bachelor party up at Red Gate. (Courtesy of Harold O. Mix)

Chop, picked John up, and went to the beach for a marathon football game in the sand. Saturday night we decided to leave Red Gate Farm to go to dinner in the town of Vineyard Haven. I was toasted and roasted to a golden brown. Somehow we ended up on top of a picturesque two-story gazebo in nearby Oak Bluffs long after the town had gone to bed. We were fifteen guys in blue blazers, swapping howlers and making enough noise to turn back the tide. Suddenly John stood and quieted us. Something was wrong. We hushed long enough to hear a policeman yell up at us, "What in God's name are you doing up there?"

Temporarily stunned and imagining all kinds of worst-case scenarios, we looked at John. He gestured for us to come close to the railing. Then, letting loose a rebel yell, John leaped over the railing, dropped ten feet to the ground, and came up running. With fourteen men right behind him. We stampeded past the cop to the Winnebago, jammed inside, and thanks to our teetotaling designated driver, Jay Budd, were gone in seconds flat. The good officer is probably still wondering today what the hell happened that night.

Frannie and Johnny at our wedding. (Courtesy of Sara Barrett)

At our rehearsal dinner, John gave a beautiful toast. He spoke about our friendship, cracked a few jokes, and claimed to have learned much from our relationship, a bond between two polar opposites. He said that our "calm, knowing acceptance of each other" for who we are was an example he hoped to follow. And I remember, too, that he said our love "would always serve as a beacon" for him.

I dated Frannie for eleven years, and we'd been married for eight when John died. In all that time, even when John and I were randy pups, he never once mocked my fidelity or questioned my emotional commitment. I think he really did enjoy the fact of our relationship and respected that I was so serious about this one thing in my life. I wasn't the best buddy for chasing women, but

John and two of my cousins, Jenny and Elizabeth. (Courtesy of Sara Barrett)

he never made me feel that I was stepping on his good times. The opposite, really: He often seemed to admire that I was in love, and he treated Frannie like a friend. As far as I know, none of his closest friends were womanizers, and as we all got married and started to have children, John, still single at that point, happily engaged with our families.

Ten

ON THE VINEYARD

———

JOHN AND I shared a belief that the first half of one's life is for generating stories and the second half is for telling them. He even suggested that I'd be writing about him one day. At the time, he was reading *Johnny, We Hardly Knew Ye,* a memoir of John F. Kennedy by his father's friends Ken O'Donnell and Dave Powers, and uncharacteristically pondering his own place in history. I just laughed at him.

We lived out many of our best stories on Martha's Vineyard, even though it was a pain to get there. In the early days, not long after Mrs. Onassis built the place, we would drive for a good eight hours in bumper-to-bumper traffic up I-95 and then ride the ferry from Woods Hole to Vineyard Haven. It was a long haul, but once we arrived we never wondered if it had been worth it. Over the years, as time became more precious and money more available, we would travel by chartered plane. Sometimes John would let me contribute toward the cost of the flight, sometimes not. After he got his pilot's license, my family got door-to-door service, right

A big slice of heaven—Mrs. Onassis's Red Gate Farm on Martha's Vineyard. (Witt Vince De/Corbis Sygma)

down to the 1969 GTO that would be waiting for us in the parking lot of the Martha's Vineyard airport.

Red Gate Farm was named by a previous owner and was situated about half a mile inland from Moshup's Trail, a winding road that passes along the coast of Aquinnah (then known as Gay Head). The name is a mystery—I never saw a red gate anywhere. It was a remarkable place, more peaceful than anywhere I've ever been. The land, which John said was about 150 acres on the west end of Martha's Vineyard, was purchased by Mrs. Onassis in the early 1980s. Ironically, she was bidding against a group consisting of Robert McNamara, JFK's secretary of defense, and several associates. John was pumped that his mom trumped the old war dogs and snagged the extraordinary, completely undeveloped parcel for a great price. He told me, proudly, that Mrs. O had underbid Mc-Namara's group but that her grace won the day.

I was probably there forty times over the next two decades, and I never found it less than amazing. To drive the long dirt road from the main road to the estate was inevitably the start of a visit even more fun than I expected. Part of the beauty of Red Gate Farm was due to the extraordinary nature of Martha's Vineyard. And part of it was due to the soft, elegant way that the buildings and the grounds had been designed. The "compound," really two houses and some playground equipment, along with a caretaker's house set back on the access road, was surprisingly unimposing. If you drove by those two houses somewhere else, you'd think, "Nice houses," but nothing more. To me, this understated sensibility felt exactly right. Especially once you stepped inside and experienced the amazing light and implicit comfort of the design. I'm not an architect, so I can't tell you how Hugh Newell Jacobsen did it, but there was something about the inside of both houses that made you feel you were being wrapped in a big robe of clean, soft, white terry cloth.

John and I visited Red Gate just after it was finished. The houses smelled of fresh paint, and everything on the property was brand-new. The main house faced the ocean, about half a mile away. In between were low scrub-covered hills, a chunk of Squibnocket Pond, and a cathedral of dunes. You could hear the waves pounding and see the shape-shifting sands from the many decks and sliding glass doors that opened up to the fresh sea air. About a hundred yards west of the main house, through a small orchard-to-be, was the "barn," really another, smaller house. The barn had bleached-wood floors, antique New England furniture, a sweet stereo, and five bedrooms. One of these was the silo, which con-

The barn at Red Gate. (Courtesy of the author)

tained a circular room at the top of a spiral staircase. The silo was John's room, really a bed with a floor-to-ceiling window overlooking the ocean. That was all the boy needed for years to come.

My favorite room in the barn was a bedroom at the end of the upstairs hallway that had three large watercolors of castles that were, to me, obviously representative of Camelot. I loved staring into and through their pastel imagery on sun-filled mornings, hoping that John's mom still had a place in her heart where she could revel in her more pleasant memories. She was the one who had coined the metaphor of Camelot to describe the Kennedy years. "There'll never be another Camelot again," she told her writer friend Theodore H. White shortly after her husband's assassination. I think that's why there was so little of her life, pre-1963, in the apartment at 1040 Fifth Avenue, and nothing at all in the main

house on the Vineyard. Because it could never exist again. That era
of grace and possibility had ended, and ended terribly. Besides, she
was too good a mother to let her children dwell in a dark past. It
made perfect sense to me that Mrs. Onassis adored the work of
Joseph Campbell, especially his award-winning series, *The Power
of Myth*. She understood the power of myth and the loss that accompanied its demise. Which is not to say that it was ever sad up
there—quite the opposite. Even on the darkest, coldest winter day,
Red Gate was starkly beautiful and almost mystically serene.

The main house was as airy and light-filled as the barn, though
slightly more elegant. It was decorated with sisal rugs; comfortable,
plump couches and chairs; sparse old New England furniture; and
a mix of art that ranged from big Audubon prints to contemporary
paintings. While Mrs. O was alive, the main house was her domain
and John and his friends hung out at the barn. We followed a certain routine on our visits, established at the start and kept right up
to the end. This routine was in itself a pleasure, giving time a relaxed but healthy-feeling structure. Most days we'd wake up late
(until the kids came along) and straggle over to the main house for
breakfast. The kitchen was Marta's realm, and her scrambled eggs
were famous, but she tolerated my big sleepy presence as I rooted
around in the fridge for milk and toasted my own English muffins
in the big stove. A window by the breakfast table looked out onto
the yard and beyond to the ocean. You could read the morning papers or watch the birds eat from the feeders right outside. Then
we'd straggle back to the barn to read on the deck, play wall ball
against the house, and listen to the Rolling Stones. If the weather
was nice, we'd head to the beach, on foot or by car, depending on
our mood, and swim and play football. Lunch was usually waiting

The main house at Red Gate. (Courtesy of the author)

on the counter in the kitchen when we got back. Afternoons were equally lazy: more reading, a nap, maybe a trip into Menemsha or some fiddling with John's Ultralight, a kind of flying machine.

Then it was time for dinner, always the best part of the day. Dinner was served in the simply furnished dining room, candles lit and all of us showered and changed. We ate at a beautiful old table that might have been a thick old barn door. Above the table, instead of a chandelier, hung two stark, Calder-esque mobiles of small whalebones that John had made years earlier with his long-time friend Sasha Chermayeff and her husband, Philip Howie. The food was superlative. Marta (and later, Efigenio) were more than able to hold their own with the best chefs in New York. (I know this from hearsay and the reactions of my tablemates, since I was always kindly served my favorite meal of burned burgers and rice.) I've tried to figure out why dinner was always so special up there. It had something to do with the setting, the company, the food, the standard of sophistication—a mix of warmth and style and civility that made your heart beat a little faster.

Maurice and Mrs. Onassis presided at these dinners, though gently, somehow conjuring engaging conversation from all of us about art, books, and the day's adventures. Mrs. O was an editor at Doubleday at that time and might mention a manuscript or book idea that intrigued her. She and Maurice loved art, and I remember a giant canvas in the dining room one year that they'd bought from a young Mexican artist in Sante Fe. One evening the topic of discussion was a question: Which two books would you bring to a deserted island to start a new civilization? I chose the U.S. Constitution and *Harold and the Purple Crayon,* a risky choice in that crowd, especially with Ed Schlossberg's *Einstein and Beckett: A Record of an Imaginary Discussion with Albert Einstein and Samuel Beckett* sitting on a table in the next room. Mrs. O, ever gracious, helped defend me against the howls of derision that rose from around the table. She said that any civilization that had the dictates of the Constitution and the imagination of *Harold and the Purple Crayon* would outlast Rome. How could I forget that? And she knew how to give a compliment. She'd say, as I was sitting down to dinner, "Rob, you look like a movie star again this evening." I'd glow. She did this with everyone, as far as I could tell. Frannie still smiles at the memory of John telling her, after Caroline's wedding, that his mother described her as the best-dressed guest at the affair. Not true, says Frannie, but kind: It was as though Mrs. O knew how worried she'd been about her mall dress and weird hat.

After dinner we'd all move into the living room, continuing the conversation and drinking tea. John held to these traditions after his mother died. Our dinner conversations may not have been quite as elevated without her, but we always talked about a wide range of fun and interesting things. Then we'd move to the living room, light a fire, and play a game like charades or Bartlett's Quotations. Bartlett's, if you don't know it, is a great game that begins when one player chooses a quote, something not too famous, from *Bartlett's Quotations*. He writes the quote down on a slip of paper and then offers the name and era of the person quoted—but not the quote—to the other players. Each person makes up a likely-sounding quote, writes it down, and hands it to the leader, who reads them all out loud. Then everyone votes on which is the actual quote. If your made-up "quote" fools the most people, you win. It sounds a little intellectual, I know. But it's not—I won a couple of times.

Because the guest barn was a small distance from the main house, we sometimes wouldn't see Mrs. O until dinner. Other times, though, she'd be out on the patio of the main house, reading and sunning and watching while we played volleyball or Frisbee in the yard. She enjoyed watching John with his friends, something I didn't understand at the time but that makes sense now that I have kids. She was always completely relaxed up there. I remember walking by the patio late one morning, looking for something to do. To my surprise, Mrs. Onassis was stretched out on a chaise, her face covered with splotches of different-colored lotions. I couldn't just stomp on by. So I stopped and said good morning, trying to think of a funny remark so she wouldn't be embarrassed. But she wasn't. She just struck up a conversation about the day's activities, oblivious to the fact that she looked like an escapee from a beauty parlor. Another time she was reading on the deck while a bunch of us played touch football on the lawn. During a break in the game, while everyone went in for water, I flopped into a chair next to her and started complaining.

"Did you see that? That was bull," I ranted, not expecting a reply. "We need a sandbox out here for these babies."

I guess not everyone threw himself down next to her for a tirade, because she looked up as though she was surprised, then said, "Rob, I so love your irreverence."

I didn't know that's what I had, so I said, "With all due respect, irreverent about what?"

Which apparently confirmed her observation. She clapped her hands together and laughed. I got up and went to get something to drink. Probably she just enjoyed being treated as a normal mom. At least once in a while.

I remember seeing Mrs. O water-skiing off her boat one cool August afternoon, smiling and skittering about like a Cypress Garden beauty, at the age of sixty! She had strong legs and wouldn't accept help getting back into the boat. She also had the attitude of an accomplished athlete, with the "in charge" energy of a seasoned leader. One day she chided John and me for not tying up the boat properly. It had wrestled free of its mooring after we'd used it for a quick ski and had to be towed back across the bay the next day. John naturally blamed the error on me. But Mrs. O was well aware of her son's game. Once when we arrived late at her apartment for some reason, she admonished John, "I suppose this was Rob's fault, too?"

Memorial Day weekend was our traditional visit to the Vineyard—a core group went every year from graduation in 1983 through 1999. The only year we didn't go was 1994, the year John's mom passed away, when we went on the Fourth of July instead. (John told me, when he planned the trip, that he didn't want to be sad anymore, that he was determined to honor his mother's optimistic spirit.) I looked forward to every visit, loving the afternoons at the beach, the warm dinners, the hours spent playing games I never played anywhere else. John's and my finest air guitar moments came during those evenings, when we'd stand on the weather-worn wooden steps in front of the big glass doors that opened the living room to the outside and strum along to "Pride (In the Name of Love)" by U2.

Spending time with Marta and Efigenio was another Vineyard pleasure, and at any given moment of the day one or another of us could be found lounging in the kitchen or out in the garden. In later years, my kids, who could never remember Efigenio's name, called him "the wise man" because he always had some startling, cool fact about the land or the sea to share. We also liked Bert Fisher, the caretaker, who lived with his family and big sweet dog, Jesse, in a house on the property. We tried Bert's patience, though, getting cars stuck in the sand and allowing boats to slip from their moorings.

John moved over to the main house in 1996, two years after his mother passed away. By then he and Carolyn were engaged and they took the main bedroom, with its spectacular view of the beach and ocean. John and Bert had a few run-ins about then, since Bert had an idea as to how Red Gate should be run and John did, too. They disagreed on how much brush needed to be cleared from the property, for instance, with Bert intent on making things accessible and fire-safe and John preferring a more natural approach. I never saw them openly disagree, but John got kind of grumbly some-times. I thought he should tread lightly and told him so. Bert's in-dependent streak was admirable, and there was no reason to war over turf that was in as fine a shape as Red Gate was.

One fall weekend in the mid-1980s, with nobody else up there but John, the wild turkeys, and me, we set out to test every single piece of top-grade outdoors equipment on the property. First we four-wheeled up a sandstorm in the dunes. Bert informed us that there were endangered plover nests there and that—who knew?—flattening dunes is frowned upon environmentally. Never again. The next day, in a tree-hugging state of mind, we walked down the beach to the locally famous clay cliffs, also the site of a nudist beach. There we smudged ourselves black and played Neanderthal games. We got stuck on the beach that weekend, as we did many weekends, spinning the tires of the old Jeep Wagoneer deep into the sandy road. The first time was the most embarrassing. John and I dug and pushed and floundered for two and a half hours before dejectedly trudging back to get Bert, who pulled us out with his big orange tractor. To our chagrin, he also showed us that in order to engage the four-wheel drive, you had to lock the hubs. We said, "Uh, thanks," and pretended to look for plover nests until he was gone.

Back in action the next morning, we canoed around Squibnocket Pond, kayaked to Menemsha through underground pipes and homemade canal locks, water-skied off the old Chris-Craft, and motored around in the runabout. In the afternoon, we windsurfed, played tennis, rode bikes, and hiked to the "love shack" that was halfway between the main house and the beach. This was an old fishing cabin with a cut-out moon on the outhouse door. Years later Bert cut John a landing strip in front of the shack for his Buckeye, a flying machine with a motor and a parachute. From this cabin we noticed a small beach on the edge of the pond, maybe thirty feet long. Bert kept a Sunfish here.

We walked over to the boat and got a huge scare. Hanging from the mast, in an elegantly made noose, was a large black duck. We figured the local Wampanoag tribe, Native Americans who had lived in the area for thousands of years, had left it. During the 1970s and '80s, the tribe had begun to organize itself with the goal of preserving its history and culture and reclaiming tribal lands. I don't know if the Wampanoag had a specific beef with Mrs. Onassis, but it's true that Red Gate lay off a road called Moshup's Trail. Moshup is a legendary figure revered by the Wampanoag, a giant who created Martha's Vineyard and other nearby islands and taught the people to fish and catch whales. Moshup loved the Wampanoag and shared with them his whale meat, which he fished from the ocean with his bare hands. In one story, Moshup warned the people of coming disaster in the form of the Europeans. But when the first settlers arrived, in the 1500s, the Wampanoag allowed them to stay, against Moshup's advice. The giant walked into the waters of the bay and disappeared forever. Bert thought the black duck was a warning of sorts, one that added a little legend to Red Gate.

One morning a big group was having breakfast when John got a call from his friend Barry Clifford, an accomplished diver whom John had worked with in salvaging the pirate ship *Whydah* off Cape Cod. The ship had sunk in 1717 while serving as the flagship of "Black Sam" Bellamy's flotilla of buccaneers. Barry was on the island, and although we never actually met up with him, his call inspired us to go diving that day. We scrounged up four scuba sets (it was that kind of place—if you looked, you could almost always find what you wanted) and went out for some underwater spearfishing. It was so much fun that the boys decided more diving was in order, specifically diving for lobsters at midnight off the lighthouse at Gay Head. I'm not a certified diver, so the plan was that I would pilot the boat.

We set out after dinner, about ten P.M., carrying about 1,250 pounds of expensive and brightly colored gear. After several ship-to-shore trips in the dinghy to load the gear, we were under way. We motored at slow speed toward Menemsha, where the harbor cuts to the sea. The night was a little foggy, and after about five minutes the shoreline disappeared. We were lost. On a pond. John was at the helm, with the mutinous crew consisting of Kevin Ward, Kevin Ruff, me, and Willie Smith. Willie, the son of John's father's sister Jean Smith, was one of John's favorite cousins. We saw a fair amount of him in the early nineties as he was going through and then getting over his trial for rape in 1991. John and I never discussed Willie's trial directly, but John went out of his way to support him, both privately and publicly, even showing up at the courthouse one afternoon. Willie is maybe the smartest in that clan, as far as I could tell: quick, outwardly cynical, and funny. Now a doctor and the head of the organization Physicians Against Land Mines at the Center for International Rehabilitation, that evening he was simply adrift on the pond, like the rest of us. Progress was slow, especially after we ran aground, good news because it meant we were close to shore, bad news because we were stuck. The tide was coming in, so we knew we'd be afloat again soon, but we had no idea which direction to go. Willie and Kevin W climbed out of the boat to look for deeper water. For a good hour—and with each passing minute we laughed harder—they circled the boat, calling out the water's depth.

"One foot . . . one foot . . . one foot."

And then excitedly, "Two feet! Two feet . . ."

Willie, his voice rising, "Two and a half . . ."

And then with a comic thud, "Two feet, one foot, no foot."

Finally the tide lifted us off the bottom. We probably should have turned for home (okay, not probably, *obviously*), but it was nice out and we'd barely left shore. We slowly found our way out of Menemsha Harbor. As we did, the clouds vanished and the moon revealed that we were a mere quarter mile from the Gay Head lighthouse. The divers went in without incident, leaving me at the wheel. Feeling sort of alone out there on the water, I maneuvered the boat in a slow circle above the flashlights flickering thirty feet below in the relatively clear Atlantic waters.

Fairly quickly, the moon vanished and the fog returned, thicker and, to my mind, more ominous. Since we'd just spent hours foundering in a cozy little harbor, I was already running "lost at sea" scenarios. I put the boat in neutral, grabbed an oar, and pounded the water above where the flashlights danced below. The beams of light, which had been moving north with the current, were becoming harder to see. Bouncing in the swells, I checked that the lighthouse was still in view, noting the compass heading in case we needed it to get back. I kept banging the oar on the starboard side of the boat until John finally popped out of the water. Yanking off his mask, he yelled out, "Whaaat!?"

Fear made me concise: I noted the things we could no longer see and said we should head in. John took one look around, said, "Okay," and promptly retrieved the other divers. They scrambled aboard with a cheerful chorus of "We're gonna die!" as the thick fog smothered the lighthouse in a big blanket of white. And then all went black. I kept the wheel and slowly tracked back toward the harbor, a good mile away, using the compass. We'd been tediously poking along like that for maybe half an hour when we saw a lantern of some sort swinging wildly to the right of us. Someone was in distress. What luck! Perhaps we could turn our ineptitude into an act of heroism.

We made our way toward the lamp, calling into the fog, "Are you okay?"

Then, "Can we help you?"

Because we really wanted to help. Alas, when we finally stopped shouting long enough to hear the response, it was not good news. About twenty-five yards from the light, which was now swinging frantically, I turned off the engine. A young man's voice called out, "Yeah, we're okay, we're playing flashlight tag on the beach."

Then, "Are *you* okay? You're heading onto the rocks."

A little girl who should have been in bed chimed in, "You're gonna ram the beach. Bee-eeee careful!"

Deflated, we muttered, "Uh, thanks," restarted the engine, and turned the boat to hug the coastline, using the shore lights to get to the harbor. We'd been gone four and a half hours and didn't even have a lobster to show for it. But things got worse. When we got home, we learned that the women were not amused. Daryl Hannah, who was John's girlfriend at the time, was pacing the porch, mad as a hatter. Helen, Kevin Ward's wife, was keeping pace with her. Frannie had gone upstairs, but not before they'd all called the Coast Guard, who were out there looking for us. We were stunned they'd made such a big deal of things. They were shocked that we were so dim-witted. They marched John inside and made him dial the Coast Guard to apologize for the alarm. But they calmed down, and soon we were all sitting around the fireplace, helping embellish the story as dawn crept near. I don't know why, but that night, or morning really, as I lay in bed listening to the ocean, I thought for the first time that heaven might be on earth. And that the big riddle of life was to figure that fact out.

Several years before John began working on his pilot's license, he managed to get himself aloft in a flying contraption called a Buckeye. He bought it about 1994. A Buckeye is referred to by the manufacturer as a "powered parachute." They say that it is "the world's safest and easiest way to fly." The machine consists of a tri-angular metal-tube frame set on two wheels, with a seat in the front and a piston motor with a fan directly behind. A foil para-chute attached to the back of the frame catches the air propelled from the fan as the machine speeds along on its wheels, and the re-sulting lift causes the thing to get airborne. It looks like the off-spring of a swamp buggy and a lawnmower. The Buckeye needs about fifty yards to take off and ten yards to land, abruptly. It at-tains a maximum altitude of ten thousand feet, can stay up for three hours, flies at a constant speed of thirty-four miles an hour—and you don't need a license to fly it. Even if the engine dies a mile up, you're still going to glide, at thirty-four miles per hour, to the ground safely. Of course, if something happens to the parachute, it becomes an airborne anvil of sorts, despite the craft's "outstanding safety record." John didn't mess around, though, traveling to Indi-ana one weekend to get trained by the company's instructors. He mastered the Buckeye quickly and loved to fly above Gay Head, circling up in the thermals with the hawks. And because he was John, he wanted to *share* his toy, urging everyone he knew to try it out. Nobody said yes until he asked me. It really did look quite safe to me, and I enjoy a thrill as much as the next guy.

Frannie heard us plotting, though, and opposed the idea. She barked at me, "No way. You're not going up in that *thing*. You have a kid now, remember?" (It was true, and I hadn't forgotten.)

We scurried around the corner, pretending we hadn't heard her. Soon enough, we were out on the beach, driving a workhouse blue Blazer and towing the Buckeye behind us. We took it out of its aluminum hutch and set the parachute, and John carefully instructed me on the essentials of Buckeye aviation. I took a simple view of things, reasoning that I wasn't going very high. John gave me a headset for a two-way radio, but I couldn't really hear much. It was better that way—I'm sure his instructions would have confused me. Really, I was thinking of Larry Waters. Waters achieved his fame, and his Darwin Award, by attaching forty-five weather balloons to a lawn chair in 1982. He'd always loved the idea of flying and thought that with his homemade craft he could hover over his house for a few hours, at about thirty feet, and satisfy his dream. He brought with him several sandwiches, a six-pack of Miller Lite, and a loaded pellet gun to pop the balloons when he wanted to float back to earth. Larry lashed himself in and cut the cords anchoring the lawn chair to his Jeep. And shot up like a rocket to an altitude of 11,000 feet. It was so cold that he dropped the pellet gun. A full *fourteen hours* later Larry drifted into the approach corridor of Los Angeles International Airport and was reported by a United Airlines pilot, who radioed the control tower that he'd just seen "a guy in a lawn chair with a gun." This unlikely fact was confirmed by the airport's radar, a rescue helicopter was sent up, and Larry was towed back to land. He was immediately arrested for violating LAX airspace. As he was being led away in handcuffs, a reporter asked him why he'd done it. Larry answered, "A man can't just sit around."

Strapped in and ready, I gunned the throttle. John stood about thirty yards ahead, at the point where I was supposed to pull back on the yoke and attempt to gain air. Shuddering in the sand at first, the Buckeye began to roll, picking up enough speed by John's position that he gave me the high sign, and I pulled back on the stick. The machine popped up like a champagne cork. In what seemed

"A [large] man can't just sit around." I contemplate the laws of physics while sitting in the Buckeye on the front lawn of Red Gate on Martha's Vineyard. (Courtesy of Sasha Chermayeff)

the blink of an eye, I was at an altitude of four hundred feet and heading east, to Paris! I looked down and back and saw John jumping up and down, smiling. As we'd planned, I nudged the stick to the right and the Buckeye began a nice 180-degree turn out over the Atlantic, back west toward the makeshift airstrip. It was really cool for about seven seconds, until I began to execute step two of the flight program: landing. I moved the yoke to the right again and completed my oval flight pattern, heading back over the beach, into the wind now. I was descending at a reasonable angle, going through the landing checklist in my head, when a gust blew from the south and forced the Buckeye thirty yards to the left. I was now in the most beautiful section of the whole estate, the large and majestic sand dunes. This was not good, because fifteen yards dead ahead and *above* me was a big, thick dune. My descent had taken

me below their peaks, and while the beach was still thirty feet below, the dune was looming, well, dead ahead. In a moment of inspiration, I reached back to a favorite old Bugs Bunny cartoon, the
one where Bugs freezes his plummeting plane in midair by pulling
back on the joystick moments before it hits the ground. "Thank
goodness for air brakes," he exclaims. I yanked on that yoke with
all I had, and in the next instant, despite a small sandstorm and a
lost wheel, I was still flying. Somehow I clipped the dune again,
hard, but managed to get the Buckeye on the ground. I was alive!
Unbuckling the harness, I dove out and kissed the sand. Jumping
up, I started running toward John, who was running along a tire
track to me. We collapsed in the sand and started laughing. John
sputtered, "Why'd you land so quickly?"

I answered, "Because my entire being was focused on one thing.
Landing."

He asked, "Why did you ram the dune?"

"Because it was there? How the hell do I know?"

We wrestled the Buckeye back into the trailer just in time for
the tide to come up and swamp the back wheels. We couldn't
budge it and resignedly radioed Bert, who hauled out the big tractor and pulled the wounded Buckeye out and home. My wife was
angry. She'd seen me in the air from the upstairs bedroom
window—she said it was like watching *Chitty Chitty Bang Bang*.
But she forgave me by dinner—we're both of the you-could-be-
hit-by-a-bus-any-day-so-live-life-to-the-fullest school—and smiled
when John toasted "his brave friend" at dinner.

Eleven

MATTERS OF THE HEART

———

IN THE SUMMER of 1988, following his internship at the law firm Manatt, Phelps, Rothenberg & Phillips, John flew home from Los Angeles to New York. He arrived at the landmark Delta terminal at JFK, picked up his luggage, and proceeded to the car service pickup area. Hearing his name called out, he walked toward the limousine the voice had come from. The back door opened and out popped a young lady he'd been dating when he left New York. It was Sarah Jessica Parker, in a mink coat and nothing else. Not a bad greeting. The lovely Ashley Richardson, a model and actress who rocked the dance floors of lower Manhattan for a few years, once visited our Eighty-sixth Street apartment wearing similar attire: an ensemble of mink and Prada booties.

This was not the norm, though. When he had a serious girl-friend, John was surprisingly self-disciplined and faithful. "Surprising" because women constantly threw themselves in his path. But he enjoyed serious relationships and was, in my opinion, always looking for someone to marry.

———

The first girlfriend I knew well was Sally Munro, whom John went out with at Brown and for several years afterward. They were great friends as well as lovers, and Sally was never impressed by the trappings of John's celebrity. She was a keen observer rather than an active participant in John's public life. Her grounded sensibility was just what he needed during his first years as an adult. As for why they broke up, it seemed to me that they just reached an impasse. There was nothing more to learn from each other. In 1983, after working for Barry Clifford salvaging the *Whydah,* John went to India. He studied at the University of New Delhi and even met Mother Teresa. Sally went with him, and their relationship was pretty much over by the time they got back. They'd gone out for a long time, almost six years. It wasn't a wrenching, turbulent breakup from what I could see. In fact, I'd use the word *amicable.*

We were living on Eighty-sixth Street when John got a phone call that sent him headlong into his next serious romance. It was 1985 and the call was from the sculptor Darrell Petit, a friend of John's and a hockey-playing hunk who'd gone to Brown. In the course of their conversation, Darrell told John that he'd recently broken up with Christina Haag, an actress and Brown graduate who'd been one of John's housemates the year I lived in Boston. I could tell something was up because John's voice rose two or three octaves in the middle of the call and he started to pace back and forth in the kitchen like a caged cheetah. He soon got off the phone and, with the look of an eight-year-old who's just won a lifetime pass to Hersheypark, ran over to the window (with an alley view) and shouted to the assembled bricks, "Christina's free!"

And then turning to me, with meaning: "The girl I'm gonna marry!"

I was surprised. I didn't know he was so interested. I suppose he didn't pursue Christina earlier out of respect for Darrell. Christina has a kind of Greta Garbo quality to her. She's a raven-haired beauty, deliberately mysterious and wickedly sexy. Wake-up sexy. Those two spoke expertly of Tantrism before I knew how to spell it. They went out for years and seemed to get along perfectly. I wouldn't have been surprised if they'd decided to get married. They were both working hard on their careers, though—Christina as an actress and John in law school—so maybe everything came to seem like too much effort. And John continued to be the proverbial brass ring for a large part of the female population. He was pursued continually by women, often beautiful ones—that's gotta be hard on a relationship. In any case, they broke up. I honestly don't know why. And by the time John met Daryl Hannah, another actress, he and Christina were done.

John told me that he was first set up with Daryl by his uncle Teddy Kennedy, who was friendly with her wealthy stepfather, a generous contributor to the Massachusetts Democratic Party. The two power brokers figured that Daryl and John might make a good match. They dated on and off for years, living together for a time at her Upper West Side apartment. I had a great time with Daryl. I found her smart and somehow innocent. And as beautiful as a sunrise, although the ex-mermaid always wore pants at the beach. She's posing for *Playboy* now, but back then she went around covered up from head to toe. She and I would discuss our favorite cereals and cartoons at length, specifically Cap'n Crunch and the Looney Tunes' Road Runner. She seemed a kid at heart, like me, though the type who was always trying to help the baby bird that had fallen out of the tree.

That's not to say that she was in any way ditzy. Daryl is as sharp as a tack, and some people found the childlike air insincere. I noticed that Mrs. O made herself scarce at the Vineyard when we were there with Daryl. I once asked John where his mom had disappeared to after dinner one Saturday. She didn't join us in the living room for tea and talk. He just laughed, in that "Don't ask" way. We ate in the barn the next night. Maybe the mother hen in her didn't think that celebrity matchups were a good idea. John apparently didn't agree—he and Daryl went out for five years.

Daryl had a theory, one that she told us one weekend at the Vineyard, that in every successful relationship there is a flower and a gardener: one person who needs to be tended and one who loves to nurture and support. Or maybe it was a joke, because we all laughed as we dissected our relationships into flowers and gardeners. The problem was that Daryl and John were both clearly, and admittedly, flowers. The joke eventually hardened into reality. They broke up in a huff following a fight at the airport in 1994. John moved out of her apartment and into the New York Athletic Club for a while until he found a place on Hudson Street. Somehow they just never spoke again. I was upset at John for their awkward parting. I thought he owed her a call. But really, I never figured them as marriage material anyway. I'd already concluded that I got along better with Daryl than John did. They were very thin-skinned around each other. Lots of tiffs and small skirmishes. John was worn out by the battling. As two actors, I guess they felt their last row was the perfect denouement. A Hollywood ending in reverse: two lovers stomping off at the airport. Cut! Print it! Move on.

In one of the off moments in his long on-and-off relationship with Daryl, John had a fling with Madonna. Not a real fling, actually, more of a curiosity encounter between the Material Girl and the Hunk. They were like two big media ships passing in the night, a night that ended without fireworks. John gave a funny account

Daryl Hannah and John were a tabloid dream come true, but they worked to keep their romance real. (Mitchell Gerber/Corbis)

of himself and Madonna in a hotel room in Chicago, stuck without contraception. While they managed to entertain themselves, they never achieved what would have been the definitive celebrity coupling.

John was between serious girlfriends when he had an unfortunate experience involving a telephone. It may be the funniest story he ever told me. He was at home, in bed with a woman he was dating at the time, when the phone rang. And rang and rang. The caller would hang up, the ringing would stop, then a few seconds later the phone would start up again. To put an end to the annoyance, John waited until it stopped ringing, took the receiver off the hook, and set it down on the table next to the bed. Then he got back to business, apparently in dramatic, noisy fashion. Unbeknownst to him, he'd lifted the phone off the hook a fraction of a second before it rang—in effect, answering the call. His caller, another woman he was dating, listened in unhappily on John's romp for the next half an hour. And she didn't just listen, she screamed in fury into the phone. John knew she was screaming because when all was said and done and he'd rolled back over to the side of the bed, she was still going ballistic, a bit hoarse for the effort. He slammed the receiver down in an instant. But as good as this story is, it even has a happy ending: She forgave him. Charming bastard, huh?

Not long after, I began hearing the name of a young fashion model a lot. John mentioned her first, in glowing terms, and then I heard her name again from a coworker of mine. He told me how he'd driven to Avalon, New Jersey, that weekend just to be near this girl, Julie Baker, who he said was from Pennsylvania and looked just like Jackie Kennedy. (Too bad Sigmund Freud passed away years ago, because I'm way out of my league dealing with these looks-like-family issues.) Julie Baker was the hottest girl on the big island of Manhattan for a time, gorgeous but also sweet to the core. John fell hard. She was glamorous, athletic, and fun. They went out, off and on, for several years. I know they were physically compatible because when I made the standard locker-room query about sex, John groaned blissfully, "Oh, my God," and closed his eyes.

John met Carolyn Bessette in late 1994. Their attraction was instant and mutual. They began to date, secretly at first, I think because they both enjoyed the mystery. Carolyn, a blue-eyed public-school graduate from Greenwich, Connecticut, was working for Calvin Klein at the time as a publicist and, because of her extraordinary style, muse. John first saw her while shopping for suits. He asked someone who she was, got her phone number, and went out on a first date deep in Tribeca. You had to meet Carolyn only for an instant to understand why she captivated John: She was almost preternaturally intense, with an electricity about her that nearly, though not quite, distracted you from her physical beauty. The qualities that John always liked in women—irreverence, mystery, drama, and beauty—she had in abundance. John knew he'd hooked the big one right away, though she put up a sporting fight.

I met Carolyn for the first time at John's apartment when they had just begun to get serious. John and I had gone kayaking and I'd stopped in to have a beer before heading home. John didn't want me to go yet, though. He kept telling me that I should stay another minute because he had a surprise. The minute turned into an hour, but finally the buzzer rang. John became uncharacteristically jumpy. Bam! In walks the hottest girl I'd ever seen in my life. Tall, bright blond, in loose-fitting jeans and a big blue shirt, she literally glowed. She said hello and turned to John. From somewhere, he pulled out a cigarette—a sure sign he was a wreck because he rarely smoked. Carolyn whipped out her lighter, a Zippo with the words BLUE EYES engraved on it, and lit John's cigarette. She told us she'd gotten the lighter from an old boyfriend, which made me think of roadkill. I asked her, pretending fear, "What happened to him?" She laughed sweetly. I learned later that Carolyn was completely aware of the effect she had on people and chose to disarm or disturb them as she saw fit. That night she chose to leave me hanging. I had trouble looking her in the eye.

My first call the next day was to John, a debriefing of sorts. I said to him, with maybe a hint of envy, "I feel bad for the dudes that got blinded by her light! Wow . . . what *was* that?"

He replied, "Pretty wild, huh? That's why I had you stay over. I wanted you to meet her."

"Meet her? I could barely look at her!"

before heading down to the Mowbray Room on the third floor for the absolute best worst food in Manhattan. He was on friendly terms with everybody in the building, particularly a good-natured waiter named Victor who had the unenviable task of delivering the barely edible food to John's table. Without a two-hour dehydrating workout beforehand, even the bottled water tasted bad. But the Downtown Athletic Club had more charm than any other gym in the city. It was chronically failing, the bulletin boards either empty or calling for an assessment from the members. In an attempt to modernize, the club refurbished the gym but still booked a singer every Friday night in the piano lounge. It was a time capsule, circa 1953, so old-fashioned that it might have become cool again had the cataclysm of 9/11 not shut it down.

Up the road about half a mile was the Downtown Boat House, a nondescript pile of cinder blocks where John kept two kayaks. The club housed about seventy-five canoes and other vessels, all stored on a big wooden rack, and catered to middle-aged outdoors-people with hippie roots. The club has upgraded recently, installing a ramp and two large floating docks, but ten years ago, you had to lower your kayak over the city's bulwark, dropping it right into the choppy water, and then scramble down a makeshift ladder onto a tiny, bucking dock. If you could get your kayak in without swamping it, the river became your playground. John introduced me to kayaking on Martha's Vineyard, and I loved it from the start. I bought my own boat in 1999, the month after John died. In his, we made a number of island tours over the years. Once, we headed north up the Hudson, cleaned and conserved thanks to the efforts of John's cousin Bobby and his organization, Riverkeeper. We stayed close to the Manhattan shoreline until reaching the *Intrepid* aircraft carrier and museum, which is docked at Forty-

The paparazzi capture a sporting moment between John and me in Central Park, John's favorite playground in New York City. (Schwartzwald Lawrence/Corbis Sygma)

fourth Street and the West Side Highway. It's a rush to kayak up to an aircraft carrier, and we slipped happily about the area, also home to a destroyer and a submarine, while the sun set behind us. John wanted to stand up and stretch a little, so he paddled over to a little dock in front of the submarine. Despite the valiant efforts of Riverkeeper, this dock was essentially floating in chum, a thick soup of stench-ridden garbage. John slipped while climbing out of his kayak, fell backward, and landed with a loud splash in the gunk. He let loose a scream of disgusted fear. Moving fast, he was up on the dock before I could start laughing. And there, looming above him on top of a high bulwark that keeps the West Side from falling into the river, was a U.S. military policeman. The MP looked confused and yelled at John, seeming not to recognize the son of a U.S. naval hero, "You can't be here, this is government property! What are you doing here? How did you get here? You *can't* be here!"

We'd get shot for that today.

John replied deferentially, "We're just leaving, Officer. I apologize, we'll be out of—"

He didn't finish his sentence because he fell in again, slipping while trying to get in his kayak. This time he went headfirst into the slime. The MP, probably assuming the slime would kill him, just disappeared. Or maybe he couldn't bear to watch.

John completely erased this event from his memory. I brought it up several times in later years, and he denied knowing what I was talking about, though he happily boasted about beating the Staten Island ferry in an incident that took a few years off my life. We'd been paddling for pizza, heading to famous old Grimaldi's, a shrine to the faithful located underneath the Brooklyn Bridge. We left West Street at dusk, hiding out from an unexpected lightning storm in the shadow of the *Peking,* the 377-foot four-masted barque moored at the South Street Seaport. It was a quick storm, dramatic and beautiful. When it ended, we headed out to cross the river to Brooklyn. We made it across in a flash, thanks to a current that was frighteningly fast. We landed on some rocks under the Brooklyn Bridge and decided to battle back right away, before it got any darker or we got any more tired. Fear can ruin your appetite. We pushed off, pointing toward Liberty Island, and started paddling for our lives. John, with great technique and rhythm in his kayak stroke, began to pull away. Still a novice, I got swept up in the chop and was literally spinning with the whirling water. I stopped working, to conserve my energy, and watched jealously as John slashed right under the bridge back to Manhattan. Then, like a cork in a stream, I got caught in a crosscurrent and was pushed west, right back across the river. I caught up to John, who was hunkered down under the *Peking* again, and testily suggested he keep an eye on his buddy next time. He said he watched me the whole time. Having determined that I was flotsam at best, he'd decided to press on.

Leaving the safety of the *Peking's* shadow, we made our way back around the tip of Manhattan. We were passing two docked Staten Island ferries when a horn blasted and the closer ferry pushed out of its slip with surprising speed. I was trailing and barely had time to reverse. John was directly in front of it, his arms moving like a hummingbird's wings. The ferry surged toward the Statue of Liberty and then it got very quiet. I couldn't really see anything through the darkness and rain. I called out, "John?"

Ten seconds later, a little louder and a little more fearful: "John?"

No reply. And then, from the shadows of the bucking swells a hundred yards ahead, a voice shouted, "Hey, Pokey! Are you coming, or what?"

"Funny. Real fucking funny," I replied with enormous relief.

Thirteen

PASSING GRACE

———

JOHN WAS UNUSUALLY subdued during the holiday season of
1993. On the racquetball court, where our most serious conversations took place, he told me that his mother was sick. And that her
cancer was metastasizing. It was the first time I'd really understood
what that word meant. Mrs. Onassis's illness progressed quickly,
and by the time I learned she was sick, it was already clear she
wouldn't survive. John seemed resigned to her fate, outwardly stoic
and relying, I think, on *her* strength to carry him through. He
didn't like talking about her illness. We stopped referring to our
mothers in conversation. The only thing John enjoyed during
those sad months was his mother's company. It was a special time
for both of them, as she tried to prepare him for a life without her
and he immersed himself in the life she still had. Among the most
important things she told him then was not to be afraid of his
name. This had a profound effect on John.

During one of many stress-relieving racquetball games we
played that spring, John told me he was grateful that if his mother

had to die from cancer, at least it wouldn't be a long battle. He said that she was comfortable with her own fate and that her comfort made him feel better. John stayed by her side as much as she wanted, making his peace with things in her presence. She died on May 19, 1994, at the age of sixty-four. John went down to the street from his mother's apartment the next morning and read a statement to the crowd of reporters and well-wishers gathered there. He read, "Last night at around 10:15 my mother passed on. She was surrounded by her friends and her family and her books and the people and the things that she loved. She did it in her own way and on her own terms, and we all feel lucky for that, and now she's in God's hands."

The funeral was somber and elegant, serious without being wrenching. There were very few tears, though lots of obvious love and respect. Indeed, it was so evocative of Mrs. Onassis—beautiful and dignified—that it felt as though she'd arranged it herself. Held at the Church of St. Ignatius Loyola on the Upper East Side, the service was a graceful and unusual mix of religion and art and patriotism. References to country, culture, and faith were intermingled throughout the ceremony—how often does that happen? It seemed to me as if half the guests were famous; actually, almost everyone was—I just didn't know their faces. The Clintons were there, as well as scores of Kennedys. I remember seeing Barbara Walters, Mike Nichols, and, incredibly, Muhammad Ali.

At the funeral, John spoke only briefly, though his few words were quoted everywhere. He said his mother should be remembered for "her love of words, the bonds of home and family, and her spirit of adventure." Caroline read a poem by Edna St. Vincent Millay called "Memory of Cape Cod." Then Maurice read a poem, "Ithaka" by C. P. Cavafy, that stayed on my refrigerator door for the next five years. (You should go read it right now—I guarantee that it will improve your week.) Watching Maurice that day, solemn and sad and the opposite of flashy, it struck me how different he was from her two husbands. Maybe at some point in her life, she decided to try someone who was admiring and kind and attentive. And she liked it. Jessye Norman, the opera star, interrupted my down-to-earth musings with her awe-inspiring voice. There is no way anyone could make "Ave Maria" sound more beautiful. Then Senator Kennedy spoke, an intimate, pitch-perfect eulogy balancing humor and substance and sadness and uplift. The funeral ended with everyone singing "America the Beautiful."

Quite a few of John's friends attended the funeral. Afterward, we shared stories about Mrs. O. I recalled the one time I'd seen her step out at night, to attend John's thirtieth birthday party. Each November, John and his close friend Santina Goodman, another Brown alum whose birthday was around the same time, threw themselves a celebration. That year, 1990, they pulled out all the stops, renting a big loft, hiring a band, and inviting a multitude of friends. John outdid himself sartorially that evening, wearing a genuine zoot suit from the 1940s. It was totally ridiculous-looking. Typically, he told me that he expected to see everyone wearing them in six months. Mrs. O came with us in a limousine to the party, which was held in an industrial loft in Chelsea. We slipped in a back door and took the freight elevator up, feeling as sparkly as it gets. I remember she was making jokes about the paparazzi and bantering with her son, seeming to enjoy the buzz she was causing. She and John danced together, to a live band of Parliament/Funkadelic veterans (though no George Clinton), and then after a while she vanished into the night.

John felt pretty alone in the world the summer after her death.

A close-knit crew. (Reuters NewMedia Inc./Corbis)

He said to me once, speaking about Caroline's husband and kids, that she was "lucky she had them . . . ," not finishing the thought. He was an orphan and he felt it. Try as I might, I had trouble offering comforting words. I apologized to John for this. I'm not as good as I'd like to be at dealing with death and mourning. Kissy Amanpour did a better job. A good friend of both John's and his mother's, she was a great comfort, even taking time off from her job to be with him. John had broken up with Daryl earlier that year, which added to his sense of aloneness.

I do think that the death of his mother was in some ways liberating, if immensely sad, for John. It left him unequivocally an adult, the bearer of his parents' legacies. And while Mrs. O respected her children's independence, she was larger than life, and her influence, so positive for so much of John's life, was hard to escape.

John and Caroline held a high-profile auction of their mother's things at Sotheby's in April of 1996. They were strongly criticized for it, but the auction had been Mrs. Onassis's idea. She was a practical woman and figured that a yard sale was a winning idea. And she was right, to the tune of $34 million. Before she died, she encouraged John to go through with the sale, saying of her many possessions, "Sell them! Tell them it was from Jackie's love nest." Which John repeated more than once—he loved her impious attitude toward her own celebrity. So after he and his sister donated something like 38,000 items to the John F. Kennedy Library and culled from the hoard the things that mattered to them personally, they sold some five thousand–odd items to the public. If my children want to sell my high chair when I'm gone, I hereby give them my blessing.

The final sale total was far beyond what anyone had expected. But when the dust settled, John and Caroline received less than $100,000 each. The bulk of the proceeds, after the auctioneers had taken their cut and the sales taxes had been paid, went to pay off the rest of the taxes due from the transfer of Mrs. Onassis's estate. One hundred grand is not chump change, but it is a far cry from the millions they were reported to have received. John felt like a professional boxer: He'd taken the hits for having the auction, given up a piece of himself, and received a fraction of the prize money. And all without ever revealing publicly that the auction was his mother's idea. In this, he protected her from the press as she had always protected him. Money is great, but in the end I'm not sure John felt it had been worth the trouble. Maybe better to have quietly disposed of the stuff and avoided the beating he and his sister took in the ring of public opinion. When he received his check for the proceeds, John looked sad and a bit disgusted. He held up the letter and said, "After all that, this is what we get, less than a hundred grand."

He dropped the letter on the table and put the episode behind him. It was time to move forward and assume his role as the man of the family. John's sense of personal responsibility, always strong, grew greatly after his mother's death. Like most people, I suppose, he was forced to acknowledge the cold, clear space between him and mortality that the loss of parents creates. Anyway, he was thirty-three years old and seriously engaged in the pursuit of career, marriage, and whatever else adulthood entails.

One of John's new responsibilities, shared with his sister, was to oversee the home on Martha's Vineyard. I've already noted his jousting with Burt. John also had to forge a new, private relationship with Maurice Tempelsman. Here, too, I think he felt the need to establish his own sense of order. The summer after Mrs. Onassis's death, my family and I were up at Martha's Vineyard as John, a little unsurely, tried to find his balance. Maurice was on the Vineyard also, though staying on his boat in Menemsha along with his son and family. I read his presence as a gesture of kindness to John and Caroline, an effort to provide continuity and comfort. Maurice came over in the morning and left in the evening, an awkward routine that indicated they hadn't figured things out yet. On the Fourth of July Maurice asked John if it made sense to have a six o'clock barbecue for the whole gang. John, maybe feeling that it should have been his invitation to offer, didn't respond. He said something like "Whatever you want to do, Maurice" and walked away.

That evening John kept all of us in the barn until Maurice and his family had cooked, eaten, and returned to their boat. We never saw them. This was not John's usual gracious way. In fact, it was downright rude. John had always had a decent relationship with Maurice. He was happy that his mother had found a companion who made her happy. And the two men seemed to share a genuine

Jacqueline Onassis's companion, Maurice Tempelsman. (Mitchell Gerber/Corbis)

affection for each other. But after his mother's death, during the summer of 1994 in particular, I think John was determined to establish himself as the man in charge.

About this time he also had a disagreement with Ed Schlossberg, Caroline's husband. Ed got involved in a project for the John F. Kennedy Center for the Performing Arts in Washington to make a film honoring John F. Kennedy's contribution to the arts. John, hearing of Ed's efforts thirdhand, was angry. It was all he could talk about one racquetball session. He went on and on about how Ed should have consulted with him, and questioned whether Ed should be involved in the project anyway. I assure you, this would not have ruffled a feather any other time. John and Ed got along well. But now, with John intent on establishing his own primacy in the family, he saw Ed's involvement in the tribute as poaching. The two of them sparred for a bit, which resulted in the project's cancellation. It was really a territorial issue, the kind of alpha-male stuff that zookeepers understand best.

With his house in order, John turned his attention to his career, deciding that the time had come to start putting his family name to good use.

Fourteen

BUSINESS CLASS

———

GEORGE, THE MAGAZINE John founded in 1995, represented an enormous gamble for him personally and professionally. It was the first time that he had ever publicly and commercially traded on his name. He made a calculated, courageous decision to invest his personal credibility in a business venture with long-term ramifications for himself and, he hoped, the country's political culture.

The issue of work—a job—was complicated for John. On one hand, he had as many advantages, in the form of connections and opportunities, as anyone on earth. On the other, there were very few things he could do that would ever be enough. He couldn't just go and be a good lawyer or work at an investment bank or even run a philanthropy, as so many rich kids do. His family's heritage of civic involvement and his father's unique contribution and sacrifice meant that John had to do something both genuinely valuable and truly *big* to consider himself as anything more than a failure.

George served several purposes. It was, first, a sincere and inspired effort to bring politics, through personalities, to the people. Kind of *InStyle* meets the *Congressional Record*. John really believed in a special bond between the American people and their leaders. With *George,* he envisioned a hip, inviting format that would bring the two attracting forces closer together. And because of his up-bringing, he knew the influence of the media and was comfortable in that twilight zone between public and private life. He'd always believed that those who lived public lives, whether athletes, actors, or politicians, had certain obligations to their public. He wagered, through the unusual editorial premise of *George,* that people would find politicians just as fascinating as Hollywood stars once they got the glossy magazine treatment.

George was also an opportunity for John to build a platform from which he might possibly move into political life. The visibility, the experience, and the message of his editorial contributions were all valuable currency for a man exploring ways to contribute to American life.

A regular feature of *George* was an interview conducted by John with a major political figure. He often talked about the things he learned from these interviews. And he seemed to grow visibly with each one. The interview construct was a brilliant idea, really. George Wallace, the Dalai Lama, Fidel Castro in Havana, and the Vietcong military leader General Giap were all as curious about John as he was about them. And they felt comfortable with an interviewer whose relationship to power and controversy was personal. The rules that govern standard interviews—the problems of access, journalistic bias, and simple understanding between subject and writer—were changed when John was the interviewer. And despite his good manners, he was learning to ask the hard questions that make a journalist worth his ink. I think he enjoyed finding out that he could do it. Even more, when he spent time with these people, I think he saw that he was capable of greatness. At the very least, he was learning about the good and bad aspects of power, and taking notes to hone his political skills.

The business of selling your name isn't easy, and John was perpetually walking a tightrope between being effective and being too commercial. He understood that magazines must earn money. And he knew that his investors expected him to make maximum use of the assets at his disposal—namely, his face, name, and time. He worked hard, learning as he went, gaining confidence in the value of the editorial and his own honesty. Savvy and unpretentious about the Kennedy "myths," he enjoyed surprising and provoking people. Approving the cover of Drew Barrymore imitating Marilyn Monroe's famous birthday song for JFK must have cost him some sleep, but obviously his sense of mischief and humor prevailed. As he said in an interview at the time, "If I'm not offended, why should anyone else be?" When I first saw the racy photo, I remarked that it was "kinda fun."

He laughed and answered, "*Really* fun!"

Under the *George* name, John oversaw the publication of *250 Ways to Make America Better,* a compendium of essays, comments, and cartoons about how to improve America offered by 250 famous citizens from across the political and cultural spectrum. The contributors ranged from P. Diddy to William F. Buckley. Though the book was hardly a bestseller, it was a clever idea: Ask the public (not just the politicians) what they want for their country.

John structured the ownership of *George* so that he put up no money of his own, a savvy move that illustrates just how much his name and involvement were worth. I wasn't surprised at the terms of the deal, since I'd already spent years marveling at his mix of generosity and cheapness. Basically, while he gave vast amounts of time and money to his friends and the causes he believed in, he kept track of every nickel. Given his largesse, you wouldn't necessarily think he kept a ledger in his head. But he did. Every time I'd return a twenty-dollar bill that I'd borrowed in a pinch, he'd sing hallelujah, as though the angels had just visited.

The magazine was launched as a co-owned property of John's holding company, Random Ventures, and Hachette Filipacchi. John earned his stake by reaching certain advertising and circulation goals. It was a good deal for both sides, especially since John's primary motivation for launching *George* wasn't to create a source of income. Thanks to his grandfather Joseph P. Kennedy's success and foresight, as well as his mother's financial wisdom, he had a portfolio of trusts kicking out plenty of yearly cash flow. He once tossed a thick bound annual report of his personal assets, prepared by the Joseph P. Kennedy Foundation, at me and asked what it all meant. After reviewing it for five minutes, I summed things up by saying, "It means you're rich for life."

He replied, "I know that already."

Though John liked being an editor, he didn't like the nickel-and-dime side of publishing. From the start, he dreaded the dog-eat-dog meetings with David Pecker, the chief executive of Hachette known for "his hellbent quest to make his magazines spend less and make more," as the *New York Observer* once described him. The fact is that no political magazine has ever made a dime, and it was no fun getting beaten up with his magazine's bad numbers. "Ad pages this, newsstand circulation that. Jeez!" John once complained after a strategy session with management. The magazine was a business, though, and Hachette was logically trying to maximize John's value. Hachette paid $80 million for more than just an idea—they paid for a man. John knew this and did what he could to make it work. He would say to me and others, "*George* isn't about me." But really, in many ways, it was. The question boiled down to whether *George* was an honorable way to use the Kennedy family name. John thought it was.

In 1999, David Pecker left Hachette for the tabloid realm of American Media and was replaced by Jack Kliger, who told John that he wasn't going to renew Hachette's contract with Random Ventures. What this meant was that *George* would fold unless John could find new backers. And John took the blow hard. It was serious business now. Feeling a large responsibility to his staff, he tried. He had several partners in mind, including Rupert Murdoch's News Corp. and the auto parts consortium Magna up in Canada. But he worried that they were more interested in him than in the magazine. It was as though the magazine was the ugly stepsister you had to invite over if you wanted to have dinner with John. It was a tough time for John, who hated flying around the globe with his hat in his hand.

Negotiations were still going on when John died, but he was close to shutting down the magazine. In the spring of 1999, he told me that he "might have to wind it up by the end of this year." The efforts to keep *George* afloat had taken a visible toll on John: He'd gained weight, he looked tired, his hair was noticeably grayer. He was becoming resigned to the fact that it would close, though. And as hard as he worked to make *George* a success, it was not his life's dream to run a magazine. He had already begun exploring other avenues to keep the concept alive, regardless of the magazine's ultimate fate, including an Internet project with a political focus similar to that of *George*. Dan Samson, one of John's closest buddies, was making plans to move his family east from Seattle to head up the venture. Dan was, in fact, waiting for John in Hyannis Port the night he died.

John's sister received his interest in *George* from his estate and sold it (for nothing, I'd bet) back to Hachette. They pulled the plug soon after. In some ways, it had already served its purpose. John had risked his reputation to make people care about politics, pioneering a trail between the country's leaders and its people. That the magazine didn't make money was no surprise—magazines are notoriously hard to launch. (*Talk* magazine, which folded in 2002, reportedly burned through $50 million despite the talents of übereditor Tina Brown.) John had mixed feelings on the subject: happy that he'd tried to make it work, upset that his staff might lose their jobs. He surprised me with a quote from Vince Lombardi one night over a beer at the DAC. Discussing the potential demise of the magazine, he used the old coach's classic: "In great attempts it is glorious even to fail." And then he looked a little sad.

Fifteen

SOUL MATES

———

"SHE'S THE BEST shot I got," John whispered to me as we walked off the racquetball court one spring evening.

We were headed to the steam room at the Downtown Athletic Club and there was no one was around. He didn't have to whisper. But John was talking about marrying Carolyn Bessette, and for him the subject was wrapped in excitement and sealed with secrecy.

By then I'd come to know Carolyn well enough to believe that John had met his perfect match. Which isn't to say that she was easy to get to know. She was both shy and fierce, skilled in the acid-tongued banter that vulnerable people use to cover their soft spots. If you saw her hanging out with her friends—most of them members of New York's small, self-contained fashion world— you'd think she was glamorous, interesting, and unapproachable. Carolyn had a quick wit and a seductive mix of manners, able to swear like a sailor and converse easily with heads of state. As I mentioned earlier, she was keenly aware of her effect on people and in control of the impression she made. If she wanted you to like her,

I can't imagine that you wouldn't. And if she didn't like you, she could be harsh.

More than anything, though, Carolyn had an uncanny ability to read people. This could manifest itself as compassion or as wary surveillance, but she was never *not* paying attention. Frannie, who adored Carolyn, used to tell her she was a witch because she could read people's minds. And it did seem that way. Again and again Carolyn would meet someone, often a person we'd known for years, and sum him or her up in a sentence. She loved to analyze people, and her insights, though not always kind, were remarkably accurate. In a way, this heightened perception was disabling—she was so aware of the swirl of ambition, judgment, and emotion around her that it became like noise, drowning out the more important sounds of her own thoughts and needs.

Carolyn had a kind of startling beauty. She was dazzling to look at, with a narrow face, bright blue eyes, a strong but slim build, and that white blond mane of hair. But she never looked exactly the way I'd last remembered her, even from morning to night. There was something unpredictable about her face that refused to stay put in the mind. Which was fascinating in and of itself. A lot has been written about the energy Carolyn devoted to her appearance. It's true—she worked hard on her looks, though she was naturally beautiful. And from what I could see, she usually enjoyed the game. I'm not sure why wanting to look good is something to criticize, since most of the women in my life spend time and money to improve what they see in the mirror. I suppose it seems excessive to some, but I'd bet they don't live in the overlapping worlds of New York, high fashion, the society pages, and tabloid covers the world over. Carolyn felt a pressure to measure up to her image as John's gorgeous and glamorous wife, and she did.

When Carolyn let down her guard, which wasn't often, you could sense something wounded about her. I always chalked it up to the father who was so conspicuously absent from her life. But then again, maybe that's just who she was. Her vulnerability, while hidden beneath a tough, funny exterior, made her deeply empathetic to others. She saw herself as an underdog—unbelievable, but true—and she went out of her way to protect anyone in whom she sensed unease or unhappiness.

Carolyn's closest friends were a small group of people she knew from her days at Calvin Klein. They included Narciso Rodriguez, the designer who made her wedding gown and is now a bona fide fashion star; Gordon Henderson, another designer who once worked at Calvin Klein; Hamilton South, then a marketing executive at Ralph Lauren; and Jessica Weinstein, a friend of many years. She was also close to her sisters, Lauren and Lisa, twins who were as talented and beautiful as she was. The three of them were not at all alike, though. Lauren lived in Hong Kong at the time, where she was a driven, successful investment banker; Lisa, whom Carolyn described as shy and brilliant, was in graduate school, working on her Ph.D. in medieval studies.

Carolyn and I had an easy rapport, not deep but uncomplicated. We liked each other by virtue of the fact that we both loved John. And we trusted each other right away to make him happy. It was as simple as that. True to her nature, once Carolyn had accepted Frannie and me into her world, she began worrying about us. She would call Frannie several days before a planned weekend at the Vineyard to make a shopping list for our diet-deranged family. Talking fast and low, without any opening small talk, she'd say, "Frannie, it's Carolyn. Which Cheerios does Colette [my daughter] eat, regular or Honey Nut? Will Rob eat steak?" She stressed over the guest list, calling once in a half-serious panic to say, "There's a lot of alpha dogs this weekend. Too much testosterone. I'm not sure it's going to work." Another time, the four of us went to the art exhibit opening of a friend. The crowd was talented, glamorous—all very accomplished. Frannie, never particularly at ease among the glitterati, immediately started looking for a hole to climb into. Carolyn watched her from across the room for about ten minutes. Quietly, without saying a word, she made her way across the gallery and took my eager-to-escape wife by the arm. She led her to a couch, they sat down together, and Carolyn proceeded to narrate the event, in hilarious fashion, into Frannie's ear until it was time for us all to go to dinner.

She was, basically, a complex and talented woman with a great sense of humor and sparkle to spare. I think she had no idea if she could handle being married to John. According to him, she resisted his proposal for an entire year. Playing hard to get? Maybe. I can't imagine that too many women would have refused John, though, knowing he was madly in love. Which he was. But she was also aware, no doubt, that saying yes meant stepping into a ring where she couldn't control all the punches thrown.

Back at the Downtown Athletic Club, over a steam and an onion soup, John continued to whisper that big plans were in the works. He didn't have a doubt in his mind that he'd found the right woman. I gave him one piece of advice, which is that marriage is a decision. I said that once you make the decision to get married, you can't spend your time longing for the greener grass over the fence. John replied, without any hesitation, "I know that."

It was hugely important to John that the wedding take place in private. Which is odd when you think of how John had lived his entire life in public. But his beloved did not want a big, elaborate wedding, and he agreed. "Carolyn wants to avoid a circus, and so do I," he told me. He loved the challenge of keeping the event a secret—it was like a great game. The only problem for John, a man with numerous friends, was that Cumberland Island, the place they'd chosen for the wedding, was tiny. A lovely, rambling old home called Greyfield Inn, once owned by the Carnegie family, offered the only accommodations, and it had fewer than twenty rooms. John was sorry that he couldn't invite many of the people who mattered to him. On the other hand, as the southernmost barrier island off the coast of Georgia, Cumberland was beautiful and inaccessible: designated a national seashore, it could be reached only by ferry, and the number of visitors was kept low. There wasn't even a phone there, only a radio phone for emergencies. It was the ideal spot for a clandestine celebration.

The wedding took place over a long weekend in September. Guests were sworn to secrecy about the event and given no information about where it would take place. John wasn't that good at keeping secrets, though, and he did in fact tell me about Cumberland Island once, saying that he'd been there before and that it was beautiful and secluded. But I didn't hear another word about it in the months that followed. Most of the guests flew to Jacksonville, Florida, where they were met and taken to Fernandina Beach and then ferried to Cumberland Island. We were flying down with John and Carolyn and another couple, so our known itinerary went only as far as New Jersey. Frannie and I, who had never left Colette for even a single night, asked my mother to stay with her and explained that we couldn't say what was going on or where we'd be. We didn't own a cell phone yet, and the prospect of being completely out of touch for days was nerve-racking.

But the adrenaline had started to flow. John's exhilaration was contagious and we were about to attend what would be one of the most-talked-about weddings of the year. We climbed into our Taurus station wagon and drove to a small private airport in Teterboro, New Jersey. There we met John's boyhood friend Billy Noonan and his wife, Kathleen, in the airport lounge. About twenty minutes later, John and Carolyn came flashing in, like creatures from a diamantine planet. John had rented a Learjet for the weekend and we whisked down the East Coast in high style, landing at a small airport in St. Mary's, Georgia, just after darkness. The soon-to-be bride and groom giggled the whole way down. We all had this tingly sense of "Can you believe this is happening?" A local hired hand with a Chuck Yeager drawl and a big old Buick drove us from the airport to Bubba Gump's shrimp dock. I swear. We climbed into an old fishing boat and motored through empty waterways and across an otherwise silent bay to Cumberland Island, reaching the Greyfield Inn just in time for dinner with about a dozen other early comers.

The Greyfield Inn was built in 1900 as a home for Thomas Carnegie's daughters, Thomas being the lesser-known brother of steel magnate Andrew Carnegie. Converted to a hotel in 1962, the two-hundred-acre estate is overseen by a sixth-generation Carnegie and local beauty named Gogo Ferguson and her husband, David Sayre. It is low-key and lovely, with a sort of lost-in-time air. We couldn't see much of the island or the grounds because it was dark by then, but it felt and sounded both peaceful and a little wild. After tossing our bags in our rooms, which were decorated with turn-of-the-century furniture, we made our way down to the dining room.

Cocktails were served in a parlor as we waited for everyone to come downstairs for dinner. John's friend Kevin Ruff, a stand-up comedian and actor, had arrived earlier from Los Angeles and was making us all laugh. John and Carolyn were glowing, happy to begin celebrating this thing they'd been planning for months. As we were all chatting and catching up, Carolyn asked me where Frannie was. I said she probably hadn't finished changing yet. Half an hour passed and she asked me again. I shrugged. Carolyn looked at me for a second, turned on her heel, and ran up the stairs to our room. She knocked on the door, went inside, and found, as she somehow must have known, my wife sitting on the bed looking miserable. Carolyn walked over, gave her a hug, and said, "Hey, hon. Are you missing Colette? Is this the first time you've ever left her?" At which point my wife, to her embarrassment, burst into tears. Carolyn stayed for a few minutes, talking away and waving off Frannie's apology for blubbering like a baby on the eve of Carolyn's wedding. Then she said, "Okay, babe, take your time," and went back downstairs. My wife made it down a few minutes later.

Carolyn's friends, especially Narciso, Gordon, and Jessica, worked incredibly hard that weekend, fitting the dress, tending to Carolyn and her family, and generally using their top-notch talents to create a beautiful wedding. If one measure of people is the love and loyalty of their friends, John and Carolyn, together and separately, scored off the chart. And the two groups of friends got along swimmingly. I remember being surprised at how close John seemed to Carolyn's buddies—I guess he'd spent more time with them than I knew. We all woke up Friday to a sunny day that revealed the full natural beauty of Cumberland Island, a place like the mythical South you read about, with huge oaks hung with moss and wild horses roaming the beach. We rode bikes, poked around the property, and kept our eyes open for the tabloid spies we imagined behind every tree. By then we were all fully engaged in John's quest for secrecy, and with each minute we were more excited at the thought that he was going to pull it off.

There was a rehearsal dinner on the veranda Friday night. It was boisterous and lighthearted, for the most part, except for a toast made by Carolyn's mother, Ann Freeman. I don't remember her exact words, but she implied that she was worried for her daughter, unsure if this union was in her best interest. In hindsight, it's chilling. At the time, I was surprised at her bluntness and felt bad for John, who was visibly stung by the remarks. But the emotional ripple was absorbed by the crowd, most of whom had no such worries, and after dinner we all piled out to the beach, where a bonfire blazed and a bar had been set up under a big tent in the dunes. Some people went to bed, others kept the party going. Although I've hardly seen them since, I felt related to Narciso and Gordon by the wee hours. The heartiest souls ended up talking in a small house, set to the side of the inn, that was serving as Carolyn's wedding suite that weekend. She, wise woman, had gone to sleep hours ago. The rest of us turned in at dawn.

Saturday, when we made it out of bed, was also spent at the beach, a seventeen-mile-long ribbon of unsullied sand and dunes where we swam and played football and watched the occasional single-engine plane fly slowly overhead. Word had gotten out that John and Carolyn were on the island, possibly to get married, and the *National Enquirer* managed to get a few shots of the picnic. We were all in such good spirits that we waved each time it passed by. (I'm the guy holding the football in the October 8 issue.) I remember Kissy and Maurice talking earnestly about world events. Bobby Kennedy and John's little nephew Jack were fishing as if it were a new religion. Ed Schlossberg did not want to play touch football.

"Hey, Ed, do you wanna—" I asked.

"No," said Ed.

"You might want to think about it a little more," I replied, getting a laugh from him and Caroline.

Carolyn's twin sisters, Lauren and Lisa, whom most of us had never met before, showed up on the beach that afternoon. They sat down on a blanket a good hundred yards from anyone else and coolly looked us over. Obviously, they weren't sure we were good enough for Carolyn. Several guys ventured over to say hello and came back smitten, though also a bit frightened. I ventured over to their blanket for a five-minute introduction and came away impressed. Though they were visibly happy to see Carolyn's buddies, they kept their distance from the rest of us that day.

Late that afternoon, John called a bunch of guys into his suite and gave us a wedding party gift. It was not the traditional cummerbund or cuff links. Instead, John gave us all navy blue silk boxer shorts, with his initials embroidered on the right leg and our own on the left. I can only imagine that he was pleased as punch thinking that we'd all be wearing his initials the next time we bedded down with our mates. The shorts all appeared to be his size, too. I held the wee thing up to my large lower torso and said, "Huuuh?"

John responded with a devilish grin: "Wear them well, my friends." And then, chortling, "Think of me when you wear them."

Each set of boxers was packaged in a little wooden box. Mine still sits in my closet, awaiting the next time I'm eighteen years old.

The wedding ceremony was scheduled for dusk on Saturday. With great expectations, the group of about forty people piled into a convoy of old four-wheel-drive vehicles and bounced our way along a dirt road through the woods. The trip was fourteen miles and took a long time. Finally we reached a clearing in which stood a tiny white clapboard church. The First African Baptist Church had been built by freed slaves many years before, and Efigenio had spent the day decorating it with flowers. We'd worried about being late, but the wedding didn't start for more than an hour. It turned out Narciso had to make some last-minute alterations to Carolyn's dress because of all the weight she'd lost. So we kicked rocks around the chapel for a while and laughed at Bobby, who was improbably chasing an armadillo through the woods. We heard about several photographers, intrepid celebrity-wedding specialists, who'd made their way to the island and been found by the security men John had hired. In the version I heard, the photographers begged to be taken away from the mosquito-filled scrub surrounding the church. We were in the middle of nowhere, but to judge from the buzz and our nerves, we were at the center of the universe. At one point a security guard yelled, "They're coming!" referring to the paparazzi. We all jumped, but it was just one of Bobby's armadillos, crashing through the brush.

At last Carolyn arrived in a burst of energy and beauty. Have I mentioned how beautiful she was? I'll say it again—you couldn't look away from her. And on that night, in her simple and flawless wedding gown, with her hair swept back and a smile on her face, we were all dazzled. So, with the night fast approaching and no electricity, we filed into the tiny candlelit chapel. I think there were maybe eight pews. Anthony Radziwill served as John's best man, Caroline was the matron of honor, and Carolyn's stepfather, Richard Freeman, gave her away. Father Charles O'Byrne, a family friend of the Kennedys' who'd presided over John's mother's funeral (and would preside over his), performed the ceremony. It was emotional, exciting, and a little surreal. When Father O'Byrne pronounced them man and wife, we all cheered.

Back in the vintage transports, the troupe wheeled merrily through the dark woods to the inn. Dinner was a seated affair held on the second-floor porch that fronted the length of the inn, with two tents set up near a giant mangrove tree for the DJ, dance floor, and bar. I can't comment on the food because there were no burgers—I lived on Orangina the entire weekend. (Carolyn had warned me beforehand that they hadn't been able to arrange for any "Robbie food" and that I might want to bulk up for the event.) The toasts and tributes began early and went late, many made by masters of the form. Senator Kennedy, Bobby Kennedy, Timmy Shriver, and Willie Smith all made eloquent remarks. My own toast was unremarkable, though it did contain the image, which John and Carolyn got a kick out of, of two folks heading off into the sunrise on a steamroller named Love.

During dinner, John's friend John Perry Barlow, former lyricist for the Grateful Dead and founder of the Electronic Frontier Foundation, became increasingly drunk. Not that anyone disapproved; most of us didn't even notice. But Barlow, as everyone called him, had recently suffered the sudden death of his fiancée, and John was acutely aware of his suffering. John took Barlow inside to talk to him. After a bit they came back out to the porch, and moments later Barlow stood up and gave the kindest, most articulate toast I've ever heard, a nuptial stem-winder that received an ovation. This from a guy who had almost nodded off in his soup two minutes before. (Barlow was occasionally in Carolyn's doghouse for his loquaciousness with the press, but his quirky brilliance, coupled with a genuine sweetness, sprung him every time.)

Another poignant memory I have from that evening is of Senator Kennedy and his wife, Victoria. I hadn't seen the senator in years, maybe not since that night on the widow's walk in Hyannis

Port, when he regaled us with bawdy tales and flawless mimicry. I'd always liked him a lot, even back when our politics didn't agree. (I've moved in his direction over the years.) But I also thought he was surprisingly rowdy for "the senior senator from Massachusetts." John loved Teddy, revering him for both his political skill and the personal strength that had helped his family so much. But he worried about his uncle, and I'd seen him wince when someone told an unflattering tale about Teddy. So it was a pleasure, that night on the porch, to see how calm and relaxed Teddy had become. He was serene, gracious, and, if anything, younger-looking than before. He was beaming with happiness for John, whom he loved dearly. It gave John great happiness to have the family patriarch so strong and at ease.

We segued from the porch to the dance floor smoothly, no broken Blahniks reported. The DJ cranked out everybody's favorites while the guests danced and moved from table to table, hoping the evening would never end. Prince (as I think he was still known then) was the bride and groom's choice of music, and every other song was from *1999* or *Dirty Mind*. We danced for hours, until, sadly, the last song was played and the evening was over. We all floated back to our rooms, drunk on the magic of the day.

Early Sunday afternoon we piled back onto the fishing-boat ferry, then into the old Buick, and finally onto the Learjet for a luxe sprint back to Teterboro. Everyone was punchy from the (mostly sleepless) weekend, John and Carolyn sitting in the backseat of the plane, cooing. They'd look up once in a while, seemingly surprised that we were all there. As soon as the plane taxied up in front of the hangar, three limousines roared up, another thoughtful gesture arranged by the happy bride and groom. John and Carolyn clambered into one limo, heading home and then on to their honeymoon in Turkey. Billy and Kathleen Noonan, the Bostonians, climbed into theirs and drove off to catch a flight to Boston. Frannie and I hopped into our limo and instructed the driver to whisk us over to our station wagon, about 120 yards away. I gave the driver a big tip, and we puttered home to the East Village.

Sixteen

SETTING UP HOUSE

BACK FROM THEIR honeymoon, John and Carolyn played the age-old game of figuring out which toothbrush slot belongs to whom. You know, the marriage thing, that series of compromises you make in the quest for fisticuffs-free living. By the time John got married, he was living in an apartment on North Moore Street in Tribeca. It was a beautiful place, though modest relative to his means. John had bought the apartment before he got engaged to Carolyn, and he'd had it completely redone, with all the headaches, delays, and cost overruns inherent to New York City construction jobs. The apartment was on the top floor of a six-story building, reached by a vast elevator that opened onto a rather dumpy gray hallway. You entered the apartment, a long, open loft, by a door on the right of the hall. Front and center as you walked in was an enormous photograph of two young black men boxing barefisted in a makeshift outdoor ring. The picture probably dated from the 1940s; I don't know the photographer. It was a great photograph, a picture of hardship and struggle and also spirit and grace. To the right of the picture was a small library filled with books and a big framed box that held JFK Sr.'s scrimshaw collection. This was one of John's proudest possessions, and the only object that he mentioned in his will: he left it to Jack Kennedy Schlossberg, his nephew. Beyond the library sat John's desk, a utilitarian wooden desktop set on two sawhorses, accompanied, of course, by a lightly stained wood-and-wicker chair of presidential style (it's the one pictured on the cover of the 2003 JFK biography *An Unfinished Life*). Having sat in at least three different models over the years—leather, upholstered, and now this wicker rocker—I once asked John whether IKEA had a presidential chair section. John thought about it for a second, knew where I was going, and said, "What a great idea!"

Then, more seriously, he added, "There are a lot of them, aren't there? Weird."

To the left of the desk, which faced a set of windows with uptown views, sat a shabby but chic off-white couch covered with little pillows. The study had a full bathroom, designated as John's, and a backup closet for his business-suit overflow. The primary difference between the main bath and John's was the size of the Kiehl's bottles. John appeared to have faith that Kiehl's, the cult apothecary, would stay in business. On his shelves were normal-size bottles of maybe eight to ten products, things like shampoo, conditioner, and various scrubs. Carolyn, however, must have feared for Kiehl's survival, because her bathroom was filled with industrial-size containers of its pricey gloop. I pointed this out to John once and he groaned good-naturedly. And then, he added quietly, "Carolyn's spending is cutting into my Prada budget. I don't know what to do!"

This was a joke. She certainly liked to shop, but she could and did get clothes for free from the finest labels in the land. Not only was Carolyn beautiful and constantly being photographed, but she had exquisite taste and a fashion radar permanently set on high. Or maybe I should say "overheat," since she bought into some of the more dubious practices of the fashion world. For example, she hated to be photographed in the same outfit twice. The horror! I can only imagine that in the realm of the world's best-dressed women, where Carolyn dwelled, having your picture taken in the same outfit at two different events was like losing a seventh-game playoff. Hard to shake off. While I teased her about this, it ultimately worked out well for everyone, because she shared her castoffs with her friends. In Frannie's closet, next to the Old Navy and the Levi's, hang some lovely pieces from Yohji Yamamoto, Calvin Klein, and, of course, Prada.

Two months after John and Carolyn got married, my son, Tate, was born. A blue box from Tiffany's arrived for him from the newlyweds. Inside was a sterling-silver pig, the quintessential piggy bank, with my son's initials engraved on the round behind, just below the tail. A true heirloom. John once sparked a chain reaction of gift giving that ended up in my kitchen. The story, as I heard it later, began when he was walking by Bloomingdale's one spring morning after a business meeting. He stopped to admire a George Foreman grill—they'd just come out—in the store window. He knew that I needed something like that because Frannie, contrary to the spirit of the vows she'd made at the altar, had banned all burgers from our kitchen. She did so because of my unusual cooking methods: I cook my burgers until they reach a state of almost pure carbon, sometimes adding vegetable oil to the madly splattering pan to ensure a perfectly crispy outside. Even I admit that it's a messy process. Hence the ban.

The gods must have been playing Aaron Copeland's "Rodeo" (aka "The Beef Song") that day, because someone at Bloomingdale's noticed John staring at the grill in the window. It arrived at his office before noon, wrapped and tied with a bow. A little note inside said that they'd seen him admiring it in the window and wanted him to have one. Even John was surprised at this oddball example of his influence. But he was psyched! He immediately had the grill delivered to my apartment. He came over that night, and we celebrated my liberation from burger purgatory together.

No George Foreman grill ever worked as hard as mine did. Eventually, maybe a year or so after John died, it started to fall apart. But I couldn't part with it. Every month or so, I'd open it up and try to repair what was frayed or loose, certain I could keep it going forever. It was probably getting a little dangerous. One day Frannie came home with a new one and told me I had to let the old one go. I did, but it hurt.

Meals at North Moore Street were a more elaborate affair, at least at the beginning. When John moved in, Efigenio took an apartment nearby and assumed responsibility as John's butler/man-who-takes-care-of-everything. Dinners were dazzling. Effy had been a part of John's life for decades, and this arrangement seemed to make both logistical and emotional sense. At first. But the apartment wasn't huge, and John and Carolyn had no need for full-time help, so it began to feel a little claustrophobic after a while. Also, Carolyn—who hadn't grown up with butlers and governesses—wasn't entirely comfortable with the system. She worried so much about the happiness of whoever was working in her house that she made it hard for them to do their job. I don't know if that's why Effy left, but leave he did, moving back to his native Portugal in 1998. It was a parting on the best of terms, though, and he returned each summer to work for John and Carolyn at the Vineyard. This left the newlyweds in need of a housekeeper, so they hired Grassa. Grassa was not as adept in the kitchen as Effy, but she was a lovely, caring woman, and Carolyn immediately assumed responsibility for her well-being. Which was maybe lucky, because John, taking a page out of my culinary playbook, ate mostly burgers for a period. He didn't dare complain too much, because Carolyn would pounce on him like a cat. It was a funny dynamic to watch, though probably not as funny to live with day in, day out.

I loved the kitchen of their apartment. It was always my first stop. The fridge was usually stocked with fresh fruit, a case of ginseng, and some dark Beck's beer, frosty mugs in the freezer. I'd get myself a beer and head past the living room to the den. The living room had a huge sofa upholstered with a richly textured Indian design and some traditional cushioned chairs with flower-print slipcovers. John had his mom's old coffee table, with a bunch of her more impressive-looking art books arranged on the top along with an array of candles. Joseph Campbell's *The Power of Myth* was there, as well as the beautiful black-and-gold, jewel-encrusted dagger. The stereo and their huge collection of CD's dominated the far wall, behind which was the master bedroom, accessible from a door on either side of the bookshelves. Flanking the Klipsch speakers on the wall, and sprinkled about the apartment's white walls in general, was John's mask collection. He loved masks and had been collecting them since before I met him in 1979. There were scary ones and hairy ones, comical and mystical, from Africa, the Caribbean, and Asia. The implication, in a Psych 101 way, is that John was attracted to masks because he wore one himself for so long, figuratively speaking. It makes sense to me, although he would have been pissed-off at being so predictable.

Anyway, though the living room was nice, the den was where the TV was. When John and Carolyn had friends over to watch football games, we hung out in the den. There was a comfy couch there and a big-screen television. In my experience, there wasn't a game viewed without Gary Ginsberg, John's unofficial consigliore and Old Brown buddy, so I picture him when I see the couch. An old draftsman's desk that had belonged to Mrs. Onassis sat next to the door to the bedroom. A passel of pillows softened the corners of the trunk coffee table during viewing times.

It took Carolyn about a year, but she eventually began to add decorative touches of her own to the apartment, starting with about two dozen silver frames of varying sizes, placed wherever she could find space. John joked that she was taking over the apartment with her "frame obsession, and we don't even have any pictures!" Which was true. While Mrs. Onassis had thousands of pictures on the walls of her homes, John and Carolyn didn't own a camera as far as I know. Picture taking had always been handled by professionals. Why invest in a camera when you're regularly getting chased down the street for a close-up? I rarely took pictures of John. It's kind of sad now, since I love pictures and would cherish photos of the two of us together, or him with my kids. But he wasn't comfortable being photographed by his pals, despite the mutual love affair between him and the lens. In the video of my wedding rehearsal dinner, who do you think is in it the most? Frannie? She hates being photographed. Me? Should be, but no—John has the starring role. And every time the camera looked his way, he'd lower his head ever so slightly, as if nodding to acknowledge its presence. So when it came to filling her frames, Carolyn didn't have much to choose from except photos of Sasha Chermayeff's kids and mine, which we mailed over after each visit to the Vineyard. I thought this was great, but John would lament, "We don't have any pictures, except of your rude brood."

I'd love to have seen the two of them with a camera and some kids. Someone would have to say, "Uh, John, take your finger off the viewfinder." He'd stare at the contraption for a moment, calling out plaintively to Carolyn, "Mousie, which of these buttons should I push?"

The Kodak would probably wind up in the trash, because John was no technophile. He actually took typing lessons when he was in law school, no doubt to prepare himself for the computer age. It was hilarious to see him with his portable "qwerty" board and lesson book—like watching Bill Gates take football lessons. Still, it took him more time to set up the laptop he'd haul to the Vineyard each weekend than it did to write his Letter from the Editor.

I sometimes think about what John's kids would have been like, besides gorgeous. He liked children, was easy around them, and included his friends' children in many of the activities he planned. He was ready and eager to start a family when he met Carolyn. She wasn't ready, though, and her early troubles in their marriage delayed the decision. I think she would have been a cool mother, protective and empathetic. When we would all go to the Vineyard, whatever assorted children were there would naturally gravitate toward her. She was unaffected and lively, and they could sense her energy. I remember her chasing Colette around the lawn, singing,

> I know a little Coco
> And she is very sweet,
> I'm gonna take her home
> And have her for a treat!

Though they didn't have children, John and Carolyn lavished absurd amounts of love and attention on their animals. They had a dog, Friday, a cat named Ruby, and for a while a pair of raucous lovebirds in a big white cage in the bedroom. But the noise was overwhelming, so the birds had to go. Friday had the life of a pasha; he was coddled, cared for, and fussed over endlessly. The two of them could tell Friday stories for hours. The dog was photographed by Herb Ritts, among others, because he was "so regal," they claimed. (I'm sure it had nothing to do with his family connections.) Ruby was a truly mean black cat that Carolyn doted on even while warning everyone in sight to stay away because they'd get hurt. It makes me sad to write all this. I'm not one to hang my hat on what might have been, but I would have loved to bounce one of their kids on my knee.

Seventeen

THE HOME TEAM

———

JOHN ONCE WARNED me not to turn my "family into a for-
tress," meaning not to let my friendships wither once I'd reached
the tipping point of family contentment. I mention this because after John and Carolyn got together, his relationship with his friends
and his extended family didn't change much. The two of them
continued to live a life full to the brim with other people.

There were a few casualties, though, exiled from the party because of Carolyn's fierce and uncompromising attitude toward her
husband's fame. Unlike John, who'd grown up dealing with the
distorting effects of fame and generally cut everyone a little slack,
Carolyn was new to the impact of celebrity. And it made her
deeply cynical. Though John might get momentarily angry when
someone took advantage of him, he never held a grudge. He made
friends easily and generally held on to them forever. But if Carolyn
perceived that someone was using John, she went into battle mode.
As a result, she made some enemies. I'd hear about it when a ban-

ished friend would call me, trying to figure out why he'd been tossed aside.

I can't say whether she was right or wrong, because I didn't spend much time thinking about who was a friend of John's, or why. I'd known him for almost twenty years and knew he was perfectly capable of taking care of himself. I do think that some of the ugly stories about Carolyn that emerged later were the result of her war against those she considered false friends. I also know that she was eerily empathetic, so it's entirely possible that she was right in her judgments. In any case, the role she took on was a draining one, and over time she found it frustrating. Carolyn used to divide people into three categories regarding their behavior around John: the "regular Joes," who remained essentially unaffected by his fame; the "windblown," who were good eggs but were visibly influenced by John's celebrity; and finally, the "freaks," who lost all self-respect in their effort to suck up to John and get whatever they thought he could give them. The "freaks" didn't last long.

Most of John's friends got along well with Carolyn and were thrilled to add this fascinating person to their lives. Our sense of the value of friendship had deepened over the years as the invincibility of youth gave way to reality. John's cousin Anthony Radziwill, who was also his closest friend, was already fighting the cancer that would eventually take his life. And we were watching our old friend Billy Way lose a battle with addiction.

Billy—smart, handsome, and incredibly athletic—had had trouble for years, almost since we all moved to New York after school. You don't necessarily see these things clearly as they're happening, though. It wasn't until we reached our thirties that we started to look at Billy's life, an endless round of nightclubs and cocaine, and realized he was losing himself. After talking with

Billy's family in Bermuda, a group of his friends decided to attempt an intervention. There were five of us in on the plan: Todd Turchetta, Bobby Potter, John, myself, and Robert Kennedy Jr., who had overcome his own addictions more than a decade before and agreed to help us. We asked Billy to meet us at the apartment of a friend, ostensibly a meeting place before we went out for the night. We had a bag of his clothes in a dial-a-car downstairs and John had arranged a spot for him at a twenty-eight-day rehabilitation clinic in Connecticut. Billy was furious when he realized what was going on. After walking into the living room and staring each of us down, he agreed to hear us out. Bobby did a lot of the talking, as we'd asked him to do. He'd had a highly publicized bout with heroin addiction many years earlier, including an overdose on the plane as he was heading to a treatment center. His story was so dramatic that Billy found his way out. When we all were done talking, Billy stood up, pointed his finger at Bobby, and said, "*I can handle it. I never did any of the stuff he did!*"

To our everlasting shame, we let him off the hook. Billy convinced us that he would take care of himself, that things weren't really out of control, that he appreciated our concern and would moderate his excesses. He used the gap between Bobby's public struggle and his own private decline to convince us that we weren't seeing what we thought we were. And so he didn't go to Connecticut that night. I don't know if our actions that night could have made a difference. But it hurts to write that we all ended up having a beer together at the Royalton Hotel. Less than a year later, Billy was killed when he stepped in front of a cab outside a trendy East Side restaurant late one June night. John went with Bobby Potter to identify Billy's body at the morgue. It was a shattering experience. He called me afterward and asked if he could come over. He needed company. He sat on the couch and looked at the wall, overwhelmed by his not being able to recognize Billy's face. With a haunted look, he told me that "Billy isn't Billy anymore."

A group of us spent July 4, 1996, in Bermuda burying our friend. I remember that John was particularly moved by Billy's parents, who were strong and gracious though they had just lost their son. Billy's death was an accident, and it's possible that he would have vanquished his demons had he lived. But his loss, and subsequent revelations about how dark his life had become in the year before he died, made us think about the downside of drugs. Truthfully, this wasn't something we'd given much thought to. We came of age in the late seventies and eighties, when recreational drugs were a fact of life. Getting high wasn't an act of rebellion or intentional self-destruction. It was just a good time. We assumed you couldn't get hurt if you stayed away from the hard stuff. We were wrong, obviously, but we saw what we wanted to see. John's attitude toward drugs was more cautious, perhaps because getting caught would have been worse for him. He partied, enjoyed the occasional joint, but never ventured into crack or heroin or Ecstasy. He was too committed to being healthy and fit, too conscientious, maybe too afraid of the consequences. I credit his self-discipline, but there was luck involved, too. No one sets out to get addicted.

At about the same time, Anthony's health took a turn for the worse. Indeed, Anthony's illness was the heaviest weight I saw John bear. The two were extremely close, warm and supportive and without the competitiveness that existed among the Kennedy cousins. Anthony and John were like brothers, proud of each other but also quick to tease, with the ease of people who have grown up together. Of the two, Anthony was the less flashy, a quiet, thoughtful man with a wicked wit and a particularly clear-eyed intelligence. He battled testicular cancer for ten long years. In the beginning, it seemed that he might beat the disease. He won Emmys and Peabody Awards for his work as a television producer, got married to his great love, Carole DiFalco, and was the best man at John's wedding. But then things started to go downhill. If Anthony was feeling poorly or recovering from some terrible surgery, of which he had several, John was symbiotically affected. He knew his cousin hated the hushed tones and tongue-tied sympathy he got from so many people. So John and Anthony continued to talk like locker-room buddies, as though they'd just walked off the field together. John would occasionally refer to him as "Old One Ball," which made everyone laugh, especially Anthony.

As the summer of 1999 began, Anthony's condition deteriorated precipitously. Of all the things on John's mind that season, Anthony's state preoccupied him the most. Here was his childhood playmate, still so young, dying before his eyes. John and Carolyn devoted themselves to caring for Anthony and Carole, spending as much time as possible with them. Carole and Carolyn seemed to grow very close. And John didn't shy away from the pain and darkness that came with caring for a dying person. I last saw Anthony over the Fourth of July weekend in 1999, when Carole brought him over to the house on the Vineyard for a visit. He was in a wheelchair and John was distraught. John died two weeks later, and Anthony three weeks after that.

On the Kennedy side of the family, John was closest to Timmy Shriver and Bobby Kennedy. Joe, Bobby's elder brother, was the one who seemed to get John's competitive juices flowing the most. That makes sense, given the family dynamics. Joe was the eldest, and so first in line to the throne. In my opinion, in those years they had their eyes on the same prize.

Outside of his family, John's friendships were diverse and numerous. His oldest buddy was Billy Noonan, a childhood friend he knew from summers on the Cape. Billy is classic Boston Irish: loyal, blunt, strong, and devoted to his family. He speaks with the purest Boston accent I've ever heard. My favorite memory of the two of them is from Cumberland Island, where Billy and John practiced an old Irish poem the afternoon of John's wedding, John nodding off on Billy's couch for his last nap as a bachelor. John also had a rugby crew, a football gang, an acting posse, a publishing team, a legal covey, a political assembly, and a band of loose nuts, myself included, on the side. Dan Samson fell into the nut category, a man constitutionally incapable of holding his tongue. If he thought it, he said it, to hilarious effect. He once nearly crossed some line of propriety with Carolyn, though, because I remember her saying, mock sternly, "Watch it. Dan! You don't want to mess up, what with Wifeswap 2000 coming up." She kept John in line, too, when she thought his head was getting too big. He was ranting to me about something once and she cut in to say, "Uh, John, I think you mistook Rob for someone who gives a shit."

Carolyn wasn't one of those wives who insisted that her husband be around all the time. Which was lucky for those of us who made up the football squad. The most brilliant message ever left on an answering machine came from John one sunny Saturday morning about 1997. He took the famed St. Crispin's Day speech from Shakespeare's *Henry V* as his inspiration. With an accent better than Kenneth Branagh's, John said something like this:

Good day, my countryman. I ring to inform you that we few, we happy few, we band of brothers, are headed to the football pitch as you lie in peaceful repose. Whilst I don my cleats and prepare for battle, let it be known that he today that sheds his blood with me shall be my brother. And when sweet victory is in hand, we shall see that from this day to the ending of the world, we in it shall be remembered for the feats we do. But do not think yourself cursed that you were not here, and do not hold your manhood cheap while any speaks that fought with us on this glorious morn. And do not feel compelled or shamed to come either, for with the fewer the men, the greater share of honor.

I was in fact asleep when he called. And listened to his message through the quilt. I made it to the park before they started.

John did great imitations of Arnold Schwarzenegger, his cousin by marriage and someone whose company he and Carolyn enjoyed a lot. He liked to tell of the time he and his friend Kevin Ruff were having dinner at Spago in Los Angeles. Kevin had to leave early. As he was getting up, Arnold came strutting in, a bit late but clearly in the house. Arnold surveyed the scene, noted Kevin's exit, and proclaimed loudly, "Ahhhh . . . I see the B team is leaving. Good." Arnold liked to tease his in-laws about their relatively puny earning power, something John found funny. He told me that the big man once said to Bobby, "Ahhh. Bobby, I think I will gross sixty [million] large this year; at least that's what I have banked so far. How is your year going?" I imagine Bobby replying that he'd saved a snail darter and two endangered bird species.

A number of John's friends became Carolyn's closest buddies, especially his beloved assistant at *George,* RoseMarie Terenzio. Listening to one end of a phone conversation between the two of them was like hearing that sound a modem makes just before it connects. His friends were also his partners in the many charitable efforts he undertook, efforts that consumed more time and did more good than most people know. He helped his grade-school classmates Hans and Ivan Hageman found the East Harlem School, at Exodus House, and his friend Bobby Potter still serves on the board. John was an active and inspirational board member at the Robin Hood Foundation, an organization dedicated to alleviating poverty in New York that was begun by his friend the hedge-fund magnate Paul Tudor Jones and run by another close buddy, David Saltzman. He gave his time freely to the outreach programs run by the Kennedy Library, and in 1989 he helped found Reaching Up, an organization that pioneered the advancement of education and training for mental-health workers. It's typical of John's modesty that I never heard a word about this organization from him. Rather, I learned about it last year while chatting through a mouthful of cotton with my dentist, James Murphy. He told me that his father (also James Murphy), then the chairman of the City University of New York board of trustees, and Jeffrey Sachs, who was Governor Cuomo's health czar, had worked with John to bring the organization to life. Mrs. Onassis had even held a fund-raiser at her apartment for 150 people. I called the senior James Murphy, who told me that John had poured himself into the effort, in the process becoming good friends with another Murphy son, Michael, who suffers from Down's syndrome. Reaching Up was and is a success story, and the health-care workers it trains are known as Kennedy Fellows. The program, run by

John and friend Michael Murphy at an annual ARC (Association for the Help of Retarded Children) dinner. (Courtesy of the ARC/New York Chapter)

CUNY, has been renamed the John F. Kennedy Jr. Institute for Worker Education at the City University of New York.

When I think of John and his buddies, I see him in his favorite shirt, an old Racer X T-shirt. Racer X was the mysterious, long-lost brother of Speed Racer, the popular cartoon character of our youth. An orphan of sorts, Racer X wore a face mask to conceal his true identity. He was a top Formula One driver as well as a secret agent for the international police who would appear out of nowhere "to save his brother . . . from dire circumstances," according to the official Speed Racer history. Eventually Racer X stops racing to become a full-time secret agent. "No longer lured by fast cars, he turns his attention to the much more dangerous game of establishing world peace," the story goes. Just before Racer X leaves racing for good, though, he vows to his unconscious brother (whom he's just saved again) that he'll "be near if you ever need help, no matter where you might go."

Eighteen

HEARTACHE AND HOPE

———

SO MUCH HAS been written about John and Carolyn and their marriage. And so much of it is wrong. Even when the particulars seem possible, the context and especially the characters are completely inaccurate. I'll admit that they had some serious troubles. They were trying to cope with the same issues that splinter most marriages, plus a few elephant-size problems all their own. But they were two good people who loved each other, and I never believed their romance would end badly. I know the statistics on divorce as well as the next guy. But I had faith that they'd work things out because they truly loved and respected each other. And when you think about it, who, really, could have matched either one except the other? Somehow these two charismatic, fun-loving, and surprisingly softhearted bright lights had found each other. There's no way they would have let go.

Right from the start, Carolyn disliked the glare of the flashbulbs that illuminated her every moment, from walking the dog to shopping at the Gap. And being the intense, passionate person she was, she didn't just object, she reacted violently. She withdrew in fear and anger, just as you would if you were being stalked. Shouldn't she have known what life would be like as Mrs. John F. Kennedy Jr.? I guess so, though she married John because she loved him, not because she longed for a life in the tabloids.

Compounding the problem was that Carolyn quit her job as soon as she got married. In theory, she wanted to be able to travel with John, who was frequently on the road for *George*. Besides, it wasn't as though she were leaving some long-dreamed-of career. But quitting right away was a big mistake. It left her, a woman with enormous energy and too many thoughts racing around her brain, without a focus outside of herself, without an independent identity. She thrived on solving others' problems, loved to be around people, and had a personality electric enough to light up the state of New York. Staying home alone, watching the paparazzi watch her, was not good for her emotional health. John was sensitive to her situation, asking the press to give his wife time to adjust to fishbowl living. "This is a big change for anyone, and for a private citizen even more so. I ask that you give Carolyn all the privacy and room you can," he requested of the media. And after asking my advice, he set up a bank account for her day-to-day expenditures so she wouldn't feel like a kept woman. But no one can control "public interest," and money was never the real problem.

The first year of their marriage was an up-and-down affair. Sometimes Carolyn would be her old self, glamorous and wise-cracking, the centrifugal center of any room she entered. Other times she seemed unhappy and frustrated, like a caged animal backed against a wall. That was the summer Princess Diana died, and Carolyn watched the coverage constantly. Her identification with the young, beautiful princess who was chased to her death by photographers seemed intense. Carolyn was scared by it all, shaking her head and muttering, "That poor woman," each time the topic came up. But she was hardly in a fetal position, and it didn't take much to nudge her from her corner. In September of 1997, Frannie and I asked the two of them out to dinner to celebrate their one-year anniversary. I arranged for a limousine to pick us all up in front of John's apartment, thinking this would spare Carolyn from having to stand in the street while we hunted for cabs. We got to their apartment on North Moore Street, and they came downstairs when we buzzed. John started to climb into the limo, but Carolyn turned away and walked over to the stoop, where she sat down. She told John she couldn't do it, she couldn't go. The limo was a mistake. It made her feel more ostentatiously "famous." I felt horrible. She began to sniffle, and I said to John that we'd do it another time, no big deal. Carolyn sat there on the concrete, looking so alone. John put his arm around her shoulders and spoke quietly into her ear. Her face regained some color and she smiled a little. Still tentative, she stood up and climbed into the limo, looking physically drained from the effort.

And then, to my surprise, we had a great time. Dinner was fun and easy, and by the end of it, Carolyn was her funny, smart-ass self, riffing about an encounter she'd had with Donald Trump's eyebrows. Carolyn seemed as surprised as we were that she'd had so much fun, but I think she just hadn't figured out what her new norm was yet. As we walked back to the limo, I pointed out the glass-half-full thing to her. She dismissed me with a smile and a roll of her eyes, saying how much she hated that there were photographers outside their apartment. I tried to downplay it, suggesting that it was no big deal and that she was "feeding the beast" with her preoccupation. But she was obsessed. "No, *listen*, Rob," she said vehemently. "They're out there *every* day. It's horrible." She seemed so tired. Tired of having to be "on" all the time. I don't know that she hated being famous (although maybe she did), but I know that it taxed her. She cared a lot. I think it was exhausting having to be ebullient and beautiful twenty-four hours a day. She'd gone from hanging out in their little pre-wedding sandbox to having to play in front of stadium-size crowds. Maybe they should have had a more public wedding; it might have prepared her for the circus.

But the two of them had many good times during their few years together, skiing in Sun Valley at Christmas, traveling to Europe to woo advertisers for *George,* and managing the menagerie of animals they kept in their apartment. In December 1997 they spent four weeks together in Vero Beach, Florida, just hanging out in the sun while John got intensive flight training. John told me it was a particularly special time for them, a great time that allowed them to catch up and find a common wavelength. Tragedy struck near the end of their stay there, when Michael Kennedy was killed on New Year's Eve day while chasing a football on the ski slopes at Aspen. John, who'd spent many a Christmas with his clan in Aspen, was shocked and sad. But it was the first time in his life that he had his wife to stand by him during a dark period, and this gave their relationship new strength.

As 1998 progressed, John grew more frustrated with Carolyn's troubled transition, but he also felt an enormous responsibility for her happiness. They lived out a complicated dynamic, resenting the demands each placed on the other while at the same time empathizing with the other's frustrations. John felt hog-tied by not being able to solve Carolyn's problems, though he had to live with them. We talked a lot about this during the second year of their marriage. He hated the illogic of the whole thing: in his mind,

About two years into their marriage, Carolyn seemed to be re-gaining her balance. Which isn't to say all was rosy—in fact, the two of them spent a fair amount of time locking horns. John was eager to start a family. Carolyn wasn't ready yet. She would, with a bit of bluster, say that she could never subject a baby to the weird, public spectacle of their life. She told me, "Can you see me trying to push a carriage down the street? With all of *them* running be-hind me?" But really I think she was frightened that she wouldn't be a good mother, that she wasn't strong enough to care for an-other human being. Which maybe was true at the time. Somehow, though, Carolyn seemed more lively, more engaged. I think she was literally fighting her way out of her depression. She often went to La Palestra, the gym owned by John's friend Pat Mannochia, spent time with her friends, and started to carve out her own space in the marriage. And, yes, as widely reported, John stayed at the Stanhope several nights over their years of marriage, including during that fateful week in July 1999. I've spent a night or two out of the house in anger, too. The thing that's most poignant to me is John's choice of the Stanhope, located quite near the apartment he grew up in. It's as if he tried to go "home" in his darker moments.

Which makes me wonder what those first years would have been like if Mrs. Onassis were alive. Of course, the mother-in-law thing is dicey, and it's possible that two such strong-willed, pas-sionate women would have tortured each other. But it's also possi-ble that Mrs. O might have been able to offer Carolyn some kind of rare, expert guidance on how to handle being catapulted to in-ternational fame. She had dealt with the same issues. And while I'm what-ifing, I'll also say that I think her children were what pulled Mrs. O out of her dark depths. She found a way to be strong and happy and also famous and private because she wanted to raise her children well. Carolyn, who always rose to the occasion when needed, would have been the same kind of mother.

There's another aspect of Mrs. Onassis's legacy that's relevant here. John was determined not to publicly humiliate his wife as his mother had been by revelations of JFK Sr.'s infidelities. Over the years, John and I had many discussions, usually while kayaking up at the Vineyard, about the merits and difficulties of fidelity, and we both used our mothers as reasons to stay true. Intellectually, he chose fidelity, but he'd often wonder, in our younger years, how anyone could be with just one woman for a lifetime. While John mused over managing his carnal urges, I'd repeat my rap that a man was the sum of his decisions. You were defined by how well you lived with your decisions, or how fast you abandoned them. He seemed to like hearing that. It was a pep talk, words that confirmed the value of the course he preferred.

Nineteen

AS GOOD AS IT GETS

———

JOHN HAD A religious side, a spiritual life that was quiet, flexible, tolerant, and rooted in Catholicism. He spoke of religion as a "personal thing," an issue that he thought was important but private. His outward faith was in the human spirit, of which he took an optimistic view.

Our last visits to the Vineyard were filled with discussions of philosophy and religion, in part because I'd given John and Carolyn a late wedding present of a set of fifteen books, the "Philosophers in 90 Minutes" collection by Paul Strathern. John teased me for believing that anyone could grasp Aristotle in an hour and a half, then proceeded to read the books nonstop. Our conversations became more introspective again, just like when we were in our teens, except now we had midlife crises on the horizon. With more experience to work with this go-round, John and I agreed that the human race's most important asset was one another. We talked about the idea that the Kingdom of Heaven might be on earth. I recall looking with him at a poem by the ancient Persian poet Rumi:

I have lived on the lip of insanity,
wanting to know reasons,
knocking on a door. It opens.
I have been knocking from the inside.

We both loved the idea that we all spend so much of our lives in a mad rush, trying to get to some promised land, when, in fact, we're already there.

I have a particularly vivid recollection of John sitting in the breakfast nook at the Vineyard in 1999. He'd just woken up and was looking solid as usual, reading the paper and scooping eggs and bran cereal into his mouth. I was sitting across from him at the table, eating bacon and English muffins. John held up that day's *New York Post,* showing me the headline that Hillary Clinton had announced her decision to run for Daniel Moynihan's open Senate seat in New York. He pointed to the article, swiped a few strips of bacon off my plate, and exclaimed with mock indignation, "Can you believe this? What, am I supposed to move to Arkansas?"

I looked up, reclaimed my bacon, and responded, "Gives ya more time to get this place painted."

John chuckled and shot back, "And you more time to learn Hindi!"

John had in fact considered running for that seat himself, even going so far as to meet with Jeffrey D. Sachs, the political adviser he knew from Reaching Up, to map out a preliminary game plan. I think he was relieved that Hillary decided to run. It gave him more time to prepare; Carolyn wasn't prepared to go political yet, anyway. John liked the Clintons, who spent time with him and Carolyn on the Vineyard, and my guess is that he saw them as a potential asset down the line. (Judging from the quotations she left in the guest book at Red Gate, Hillary could play a fine game of Bartlett's.)

Our political and metaphysical ramblings were interrupted that afternoon when John accidentally grounded himself. It was the Saturday night of Memorial Day weekend 1999, and I was watching the fourth quarter of a Knicks game. John had decided to take the Buckeye up for a sunset spin. I helped him pull out the machine and spread the chute on the lawn to the left of the main house. That was where John usually took off from, though it wasn't a large enough spot for a landing. I was thinking of taking a little flight myself and planned to drive to the beach to meet John and, hopefully, evade the wife's scrutiny.

Everything was in order. John checked the wind, gunned the engine, and began to accelerate across the lawn toward an incline in the terrain, just past where his wheels would leave the ground. His chute filled properly and up he went. I'd seen this countless times before and didn't think much about it until a big gust of wind blew the Buckeye a good fifteen feet to the right and into a gnarly-looking shrub. I was on the other side of the house and heard a crash. I ran to see if John was all right and found that my daughter, Colette, had gotten there first. John was slumped in the seat's harness, but he looked up when he heard Colette's little voice yelling, "John got hurt!"

He smiled, obviously not wanting to scare her, and said, "Hey, Coco! I'm fine! Just a little accident. Nothing to worry about."

In fact, his ankle was crushed and his head was throbbing from the crash. He wrestled off his helmet, joking with the now-assembled crowd of children that he needed a smaller head. Carolyn and I took him to the emergency room, where Linda, the wife of caretaker Bert Fisher, was the nurse on duty. The doctors determined that John needed surgery, which took place in New York the following week.

Heading back home from the hospital, John was in a particularly bad mood. An intensely physical person, he hated being incapacitated in any way. No doubt, he was thinking about all the things he wouldn't be able to do for the next few weeks. On the drive back, I suggested that maybe he should take this as a chance to slow down, to cut back on some of the many demands on his time. I told him he should try sitting on the couch for a few weeks, as I often did—he had no idea how satisfying it could be. I worried that he was under a lot of stress, especially with the future of *George* up in the air. John suffered from Graves' disease, a thyroid disorder, for which he took iodine supplements and ginseng. He'd hurt his hand on a broken champagne flute in the sink the previous winter. Now this. I told him he was pushing himself too hard. "No shit," he muttered.

Effy held dinner that night until we got home from the hospital. While his friends felt sympathy for John, we were also happy to be sitting around our favorite table, awaiting another of Effy's dinners—this time, swordfish. John was quiet, but the rest of us chattered noisily. I was served my usual big, luscious burned burger and noticed Carolyn, who was sitting to my right, eyeing it greedily. I moved it to the left side of my plate. But as soon as I looked away, she grabbed it and took a huge bite. Secretly pleased to have another culinary misfit on the island, I offered her the rest. But no, she handed it back to me and called out politely to Efigenio. I rarely saw Carolyn ask anything of Effy, but that night she said, "Effy, would you mind making me one of those delicious hamburgers?"

Efigenio, surprised but amused, replied, "Of course not, how would you like it?"

"Rare. Bloody. Please."

I'm proud to say that on our next visit, a month later, Carolyn had dispensed with the gourmet menu entirely and was subsisting on pink burgers each night. She wolfed them down with the appetite of a linebacker.

That summer we spent both Memorial Day and the Fourth of July on the Vineyard with John and Carolyn, flying up in John's shiny new red Piper Saratoga. There was a flight instructor on board both times, but John was at the controls the whole time. His landings were barely noticeable, something he took pride in. None of us felt nervous about flying with John—he was the opposite of reckless, with the attitude of a cautious and serious pilot. Although he mentioned that his new plane was more aerodynamically sensitive than his previous Cessna— "squirrelly" was his word—our four flights that summer were perfect.

The Fourth of July visit was an unexpected one, a last-minute invitation that came about because Carolyn told John she'd had so much fun on Memorial Day that she wanted to do it again. We usually spent the holiday at the beach in New Jersey, but our rental started later that year and we gladly accepted their invitation. I am forever grateful to Carolyn for that last visit. It was a gorgeous and fun-filled weekend, everyone relaxed and happy to be together. When it was over, on Monday night, we said good-bye to Carolyn, who was staying to help Anthony move to Red Gate for the rest of the month. John flew us back to the airport in Caldwell, New Jersey. That's where we last saw each other. He had to stay to fill out some paperwork and clean and put the plane away, so we said our good-byes standing behind the right wing on the tarmac. Filled with memories of the wonderful weekend we'd just had, we leaned into each other and shared a hug and a handshake. I said, stating the obvious, "That worked out nicely."

John responded, "As good as it gets."

Two weeks later, my wingman left my side forever. My silver lining, though inadequate, is that at least we went out on top.

Twenty

SAD DAY

———

ON THE NIGHT of July 16, 1999, John's plane crashed into the ocean off the coast of Martha's Vineyard. John, Carolyn, and Carolyn's sister Lauren were killed. I was at a family reunion in New Jersey that weekend, staying at a small resort with my stepfather, David Katz, and his children. David, an early riser, literally ran into the condominium where we were staying and told Frannie what he'd just seen on television. She woke me with the news that John's plane was "missing," as it was being reported at the time. My first reaction was to curl up in a ball, as tightly as possible, and just not *be*. I stayed like that, clenched like a fist, for a while. Then I jumped out of bed, unsure what to do but desperate to move.

Although the news reporters were saying that the plane had disappeared from radar over the Atlantic Ocean, I had no hope. None. I struggled to block out the horrible images that were flooding my mind. But there were no generalities to hide in: I knew the inside of the plane, I knew the route, I knew John so well that I could barely breathe at the thought of what had happened. I stumbled out into the living room and my mom jumped up to turn off the TV. My kids, five and almost three years old then, understood that something terrible was happening. I walked over and hugged both of them before standing with my arms around Frannie for a moment, silent but sharing our sadness.

I remember thinking that grief was directly related to love and friendship, that it's a twisted irony that two of life's greatest pleasures have such a cost. I was angry at John for leaving me. And I felt diminished, smaller than I'd been the day before. I love to connect to people, maybe above all else, and the man I'd gotten closer to than anyone had been ripped away. John was my biggest fan, my ally in the war of life. He was a great strength to me, and I to him. And though we'd joked for twenty years about who would outlive the other, we never planned on dying young.

Determined to erase the pictures from my brain, I tried to conjure up other, more comforting possibilities. I imagined, though I didn't believe it, that they were hiding somewhere. I told Frannie that the three of them were probably sitting on No Mans Land, a tiny island off the Vineyard that was used for military target practice. John was getting ready to cook up some endangered plover eggs for breakfast.

I dressed in a daze, feeling as though I was choking in the airless condo with my family looking at me worriedly. The resort we were staying at was at the foot of a little mountain, and without thinking, I walked out the door and started to climb. It felt like something John would do—go outside, be in Nature, climb a mountain. I was practically running by the time I reached the top. I stayed there for a moment, then headed back, leaping and sliding down the gravelly trail as John and I had done together in Ireland. About halfway down, something—my mind? my body? my friend?—

came to my rescue. I stopped on the hill and felt a presence to my right. And John told me, "It's okay, Rob. I'm all right."

I knew that this vision—because that's what it felt like, a vision—was in my mind, but it was powerful just the same. John's spirit, which lives within me and everyone else who loved him, felt utterly real, like something I could hear and feel and touch. And despite my total disbelief in the supernatural, I trusted this. My unspeakable fear, that John and Carolyn and Lauren had suffered pure, unimaginable terror as their plane went into an irrecoverable dive, was allayed. John told me that he was okay that morning on the hill, and I hold it as true.

For reasons I don't fully understand, John's and Carolyn's ashes were ceremoniously tossed into the Atlantic from a U.S. Navy ship, the USS *Briscoe,* off the Massachusetts coast near Martha's Vineyard. Only close family attended the ceremony. John wasn't in the navy, he wasn't a seaman, and he didn't live in Massachusetts. There is no place to go and pay tribute to and reflect upon John. (Though when I go swimming at the Jersey Shore each summer, I figure that, in some logarithmically infinitesimal way, we're swimming together.)

The next week is blurry in my memory. The television and the newspapers carried endless news, but there was no real news. I stopped listening or reading. The whole world was mourning my friend, which I guess is weird but seemed completely right. John's many friends began to arrive in the city and seek out one another. Randy Poster, a friend from Brown who'd moved to Los Angeles, hosted a gathering of John's acting buddies. Maura, the sister of John's artist friend Sasha, had a bunch of old New York friends over, a mix that he'd met from grade school to grad school. There was a dinner held by the *George* gang at Café Loup on Thirteenth

The USS *Briscoe* carrying the ashes of John and Carolyn and Lauren Bessette to a burial at sea off Martha's Vineyard on July 22, 1999. (Courtesy of Corbis)

Street. John meant so much to so many people. And none of us had ever considered that he wouldn't be a part of our lives for the duration. The loss and the shock were enormous. So we all gravitated to one another, looking to console ourselves in the connections we had to him. It was uplifting, because it felt as if John's presence was amplified when we were together.

The memorial service for John and Carolyn was beautiful, probably the first time in my life I understood the consoling power of rituals like funerals. The logistics of the service were taken care of by Teddy's office. On Thursday I received a call from a staff member informing me that I was a pallbearer. That was the word, though there was no casket. Within the hour a clean-shaven young man showed up at my door with invitations for Frannie and me, small cards that we needed to get through several security checkpoints.

Friday was warm and sunny and we took a cab uptown about
ten A.M., walking the last few blocks to the Church of St. Thomas
More, on East Eighty-ninth Street, through throngs of people
who'd come to pay their respects. The service itself was sad, but
not unbearably so. I'm not sure why. Maybe we'd exhausted our
tears. Or maybe, where Carolyn and John were concerned, there
was solace in knowing they'd died together. No doubt, Teddy
Kennedy, so sadly accustomed to burying his beloved family members, knew how to guide us. He gave a moving and powerful eulogy, filled with humor as well as warmth. And there was the fact,
which John's friends talked about later, that he would have been
devastated to see people so sad on his account. The most difficult
moment was when Ann Freeman, Carolyn and Lauren's mother,
somehow found the superhuman strength to stand and read from a
book called the *Facts of Faith*. I can't fathom how she did it. Caroline read from Shakespeare's *The Tempest*, which John had performed in. The sight of these bereaved family members acting with
such strength straightened my spine. Near the end of the service,
Wyclef Jean sang "Many Rivers to Cross," the melancholy, faith-
infused Jimmy Cliff song. As his voice filled the vaulted apses, I
felt a wave of sadness wash over me, but I also sensed something
transcendent that was beauty or love or spirit. I didn't want the
song to end. I wanted to hold on to that hopeful moment. But it
ended, and as the music finished, the other pallbearers and I, with
no casket to carry, began to cry.

There was a reception right after the funeral, held at the Con-
vent of the Sacred Heart, a few blocks away. It was a quiet affair,
not tearful but resigned. Our good-byes were made somewhat easier by the reunion of so many of John's closest friends. We told
stories, shared how we were coping, wondered if we'd ever see one

another again. People laughed—we all had too many happy memories of John and Carolyn not to smile sometimes. Besides, it was hard not to believe that John was watching us that day, deeply sorry for our grieving and smiling at our good-natured quips. As the crowd slowly thinned out, John's friends lingered. We sat around a couple of tables and drank orange juice and vodka, knowing that John had collected us, in a way, and sensing an esprit de corps because of it. I remember only a few conversations clearly from that day. One was with Caroline, whom I sought out immediately. We had not been close, but I desperately wanted to talk to her. I found her and expressed my condolences, saying, "Caroline, I'm so terribly sorry. Your brother loved you so much." She replied, "Thank you, Rob. John loved you." Six words. They still fill my cup five years later.

I spoke with Efigenio, too, who told me he'd had a vision similar to mine. It happened a day or two after the crash. He said that he was driving along the sandy road that leads from the beach to the house at Red Gate. Something caught his eye at the edge of one of the ponds. When he got closer, he saw that there were words and names etched in the sand. The words were "We are okay." The names were John, Jackie, Carolyn, and Lauren. I didn't ask him any questions, just added his words to my comfort.

That night Pat Mannochia arranged a less formal memorial at his huge gym, La Palestra. It was a big group, including many grieving friends who hadn't been invited to the church. Some were angry, others sad, that they hadn't made "the list." But no one was completely surprised. John's celebrity had always been a complicating factor, in death as in life. Pat's gathering let us, friends who felt like our own kind of family, mourn and also enjoy our memories. It wasn't a tearful event, more like a party with an overlay of sad-

ness. As always, everyone told lots of stories. I remember the actor
Nick Chinlund telling how he and John had gone to a Knicks
game. Nick had played basketball at Brown and was excited that
he'd be courtside at the Garden. But John had brought the wrong
tickets with him, so they were turned away from the front row and
ended up in the dreaded "blues" high atop the arena. Kissy Amanpour spoke movingly about both John and Carolyn, and John Hare
did the same. I finished up the speeches by suggesting that the Irish
tradition of cutting down a tree when a life has been cut short
didn't apply in this case. That's because John had lived life so large
and in such an intimate, fulfilling way. As midnight passed, I
found myself sitting with Kissy and her husband, Jamie Rubin,
Billy Noonan, Santina, and Dan Samson. We all knew one another
because of John, and we marveled at his ability to sew us all together over the years.

The next day in Greenwich, there was a service at an Episcopal
church for Lauren Bessette. To me, this seemed an infinitely sadder
event. Lauren's many friends, some who had come from halfway
around the world, looked stricken and numb. There in the church,
with her parents and sister, Lauren's death seemed without conso-
lation. Again, Ann Freeman was calm and gracious, talking to each
of us after the service. She made a point of asking everyone to keep
in touch with her and Lisa, her surviving daughter. Lisa was
equally generous, though she had to struggle with the fearsome
bubble we created around her with our profound unease. What do
you say to a woman who has just lost her sisters? It was a heartsick
evening and, for those of us who didn't know Lauren well, unre-
lieved even by memories of her.

The idea that John was to blame floated in the air that night.
Not officially—there were prayers said for Carolyn and for John—

and not in the open-hearted manner of Mrs. Freeman and Lisa. But it was there just the same. An old friend of mine from Brown, someone I'd once been close to, made the charge explicitly. He'd never been particularly friendly with John. But in the small world we all live in, he and his wife had become dear friends with Lauren while they all lived in the Far East and London. He walked up to me that night and said bitterly, "Your friend killed my friend."

I'm sure he spoke from some place of overwhelming sadness, but I refused to accept his words. I puffed up and replied angrily, "What did you just say?" not believing that he'd continue.

In fact, he did, saying, "If John weren't so reckless, Lauren would still be alive."

I wanted to punch him, but I quoted Carolyn instead: "Live your own life, man."

In the years since John, Carolyn, and Lauren died, there have been constant attempts to blame someone for the crash. I've read that Carolyn was to blame, because she demanded a new coat of toenail polish during a pedicure, which made them late. I've read that Lauren held the group up. And, endlessly, I've heard that John was reckless. Why this blamefest? Will it bring them back? Does anyone feel better for the exercise? For the record, I'm sure John would have accepted responsibility for what happened. He was at the controls. And he was a deeply responsible person. I imagine his last thought was a bottomless remorse for harming his beloved wife and her sister. But I also know that accidents happen, even to conscientious people. And John was a careful pilot, trained and thorough and doing something he'd done many times before.

I need to emphasize this: John was not a reckless man. On his own, especially in his youth, he pushed himself far, seeking the limits of his courage. He had to. Given his father, his family, his own determination to be something more than the name he was born with, how could he not? There's an aircraft carrier and a space center that share his name. He'd inherited a free lifetime subscription to *Aviation Week Space Technology* from the commander in chief of the U.S. armed forces, his father. He was not going to be content playing golf. John also studied long and hard to master whatever skills would let him explore the natural world that he loved so much: He was a certified diver, an experienced camper, a masterful swimmer and skier. Yes, he loved adventure. His privileged life afforded him opportunities to do things most people can't: go heli-skiing and white-water rafting and kayaking. But regular people learn to fly planes, climb mountains, search for undersea wrecks—and nobody calls them reckless until something goes wrong. I was with John on some of his thrill-seeking adventures, and he was as disciplined and careful as they come. He followed the rules, knowing that diligence and respect are the keys to mastery.

I understand that John made a fatal error that night in his plane. And I also understand, from everything I've read, that this error was something that can happen even to experienced pilots. According to the final accident report issued by the National Transportation Safety Board (NTSB), he did what he was supposed to do. Before takeoff, he "obtained weather forecasts for a cross-country flight, which indicated visual flight rules (VFR) conditions with clear skies and visibility that varied between 4 to 10 miles along his intended route." During his flight, the report states, "airports along the coast reported visibility between 5 and 8 miles." And "in the 15 months before the accident, the pilot [John] had flown either to or from the destination area about 35 times. The pilot flew at least 17 of these flight legs without a CFI [certified flight instructor] on board, of which 5 were at night." Stated simply, the skies were reported clear and this was his milk run. There was no indication of trouble. None. However, the report notes that "pilots flying similar routes on the night of the accident reported no visual horizon while flying over the water because of haze." As John's plane neared his destination, this haze, together with the darkness, left him in a dark gray envelope, oriented to nowhere. The result of losing the horizon is spatial disorientation—you can't tell up from down or right from left. Spatial disorientation is like being very dizzy, and you have almost no time to recover before the plane is out of control. The instruments don't matter. Being in a squirrelly plane doesn't matter. You're screwed. In the NTSB's words, "spatial disorientation . . . is regularly near the top of the cause/factor list in annual statistics on fatal aircraft accidents." The haze that snuck up on John was not on the radar, not reported on the radio, and not in the weather reports. From what I can tell, they got bushwhacked.

While researching John's final flight, I found this coincidental NTSB report: "On March 30, 2000, about 2025 Eastern Standard Time, a Boeing 767-332, operated by Delta Airlines as flight 106," took off from John F. Kennedy International Airport. The plane was headed to Frankfurt, Germany, with 225 people on board. As it was making its climb from the airport, with the first officer flying and the autopilot not engaged, the airplane suddenly rolled to the right. The pilot grabbed control of the plane, dumped twenty thousand pounds of fuel, and returned safely to Kennedy. What had happened was that the first officer had lost control of the plane, telling the NTSB "there was no horizon, stars, or moon, and all he saw was darkness." The report noted that "the first officer's failure to maintain control of the airplane . . . was a result of spatial disorientation. Factors in the incident were the cloud layer and dark night." Just like for John. But the first officer was an experienced pilot with nine thousand total flight hours for Delta and training in both the T-38 and F-15 aircraft when he'd been an officer in the air force.

I'll believe in Moshup's curse long before I buy into any kind of Kennedy curse. John enjoyed adventure, but he was neither naive nor rash. He was brave but deliberate, someone who lived his life to the fullest—with more opportunity than most—without forgetting that every action has a consequence. His number came up short that night in July. His luck and preparation—you need both—failed him, and Carolyn and Lauren, too. And yet, without the hindsight of what happened, I can't think of a single reason why I wouldn't have gotten on the plane with him that night with my family.

Twenty-one

LIVE FOR THE DAY

———

IN THE FALL of 1998, John told an interviewer that "the beginning of life is just preparation." It wasn't hyperbole: John had consciously spent his years preparing to be of service and value to his country. But before the curtain rose on Act Two, the lead actor left the building.

He'd begun his efforts with *George*. His next goal was to be a New York senator, or possibly governor. And then he would have run for President. Maybe the election of 2012. That morning on the Vineyard when we joked about my needing to work on my Hindi, I asked John how much time I had. He responded laughingly, "How about 2012? Unless you need more time, of course." It was only partly a joke. In 2012 John would have been fifty-two. He'd already been offered the opportunity to run for Senator Lautenberg's seat in New Jersey, presumably using his mom's Peapack address as his home base. He'd rejected that idea but had begun to put a team together to develop a road map for his political future.

John was intensely dedicated to his destiny, and he had his nose quietly to the grindstone.

John had the potential to do great things. He embodied a unique convergence of factors: a good and smart person born with extraordinary access and real power, endowed with the trust and goodwill—both inherited and earned—of most of the world. His entire short life, he worked diligently to turn all that he'd been born with into something of value. I'd bet the ranch he would have been President, but there were other jobs he could have done well, too. We used to puzzle over what President Clinton would do after his second term ended, since he was relatively young to be retired from the top of the world's biggest totem pole. John mentioned that the United Nations had never had an American secretary-general. It's a thought.

I used to tell my wife—because I couldn't really tell anyone else—that John would be there when his country needed him. He wasn't there when the Twin Towers fell, though that day made me understand much more clearly what exactly he could have contributed. John had a worldly and inclusive vision of America, a deep patriotism that was nonetheless open-hearted and sophisticated about the connectedness of the world's nations. In this he was like his father, who in a speech not long after World War II spoke of the world's need to "recognize how interdependent we are." He had a motley and marvelous pantheon of heroes, including Abraham Lincoln (John loved the quote "Am I not destroying my enemies when I make friends of them?") and Mustafa Atatürk, the brilliant general who defeated the Allied powers at Gallipoli in World War I and went on to turn Turkey into a modern, democratic, secular state.

Back when we first got out of school, I was a little afraid of

John's future as a politician. I worried I'd lose touch with him. Personally, I'd have been happy just to grow old with him, a not-quite-average citizen who was my dear friend. (Though I would have made a fine ambassador.) Not long after the crash, someone asked me what I was going to do without the sparkle and glamour he brought to my life. No more courtside tickets at Knicks games. No more paparazzi shots of the two of us in the *New York Post*. I was offended, but actually it was a fair question. Certainly I knew and loved John outside of his fame. But it's also true that my day-to-day life is very different without him. No special access, no trips to the Vineyard, no flashbulbs. I'd be a liar if I said I didn't miss that—it was fun, especially because it was with John.

For a long time after John died, I couldn't figure how to fill the emotional void he'd left in my life. My kids made me happy, and I had good friends who stayed close. But nothing was as much fun. I didn't go out much. I've always been big on counting my blessings, and I do, but I was deeply angry. And there wasn't a single thing I could do about it, of course. People are not replaceable. Besides, it's not as though you can grow up with someone when you're already grown. Knocked off my horse, I sat on the ground for a while. Two years later I turned forty. The one-two punch sent me reeling. Not a religious person, I decided I needed some kind of spiritual center. The heaven on earth thing needed some work. I started working on a book, not finished yet, about God and man and all the things John and I had debated for years. It was a good thing to do, one that led me here, to this book about my friend.

I wrote a book and I bought a kayak and I work out daily. You put pieces of your friends inside you. As I realized even that morning of John's crash, love and loss go together. I still think it's important to understand what might have been. In *Johnny, We Hardly*